# Gameful Project Management

## Self-Gamification Based
## Awareness Booster
## for Your Project Management Success

Book 1

in Series

"Gameful Life"

# Victoria Ichizli-Bartels

# Gameful Project Management
## Self-Gamification Based Awareness Booster for Your Project Management Success
### Book 1 in Series "Gameful Life"
#### 1st Edition

Cover design by Alice Jago

The sources to the quotations made in the book are given before, after, or in the same places as the quotes in the text.

Optimist Writer

For my sister Svetlana,
*One of the most passionate project managers*
*I've ever met.*

# Table of Contents

# Three Quotes Instead of a Preface

***

"Lessons learned in games have a greater impact
than lessons learned any other way."
— Richard Garfield

***

"Anyone who tries to make a distinction between
education and entertainment doesn't know the first
thing about either."
— Marshall McLuhan

***

"Work is actually very similar to play and even
more like games. The main difference is
perception."
— Andrzej Marczewski

# More on Self-Gamification

The resources listed here are those available at the time of publishing. For the full list of available resources on Self-Gamification, which grows continually, go to www.victoriaichizlibartels.com/Self-Gamification/

**Books**
*Self-Gamification Happiness Formula* addresses Self-Gamification in detail. You can check it out here: www.victoriaichizlibartels.com/Self-Gamification-book/

*5 Minute Perseverance Game* is a short, fun book, which I wrote before I had heard about gamification and kaizen, two of the approaches Self-Gamification brings together. I invite you to check it out here: www.victoriaichizlibartels.com/5-minute-perseverance-game/

**Online course**
*Motivate Yourself by Turning Your Life Into Fun Games* is an online course on Udemy with a couple of hours of content on Self-Gamification, a unique self-help approach uniting anthropology, kaizen,

and                                     gamification.
www.udemy.com/course/motivate-yourself-by-
turning-your-life-into-fun-
games/learn/lecture/10505042#overview

## Self-Gamification community
To find out how you can join, go to this link:
www.victoriaichizlibartels.com/community/.

# Gameful Life Series and Why I'm Starting with Project Management

**Reading time: 4 minutes**

I've turned all aspects of my life into games for several years now. The resonance of this, and a continued interest in what I do, inspire me to create more on the topic. The book I wrote prior to this one was the *Self-Gamification Happiness Formula*, which was published in June 2019.

I am thrilled with the positive feedback I've received, and in the interest people have shown in the book and the Self-Gamification approach.

Both *Self-Gamification Happiness Formula* and its predecessor *5 Minute Perseverance Game* emphasize the fact that you can turn anything into fun games. The former describes the art of turning our lives into games (Self-Gamification) in detail, and the latter introduces a simple Self-Motivational Game framework for one project.

I often get questions about the various specific case studies of Self-Gamification. And although *Self-*

*Gamification Happiness Formula* contains a myriad of examples, there is no distinction between the areas of its application.

Which is why I am starting a book series called "Gameful Life" — because that is what Self-Gamification truly is: the art of approaching our lives gamefully.

The books in this series will vary in their structure and genre. Some will be purely non-fiction, like this one. Others will either be a mixture of memoir and parable[1] or strictly fictional but including lessons from Self-Gamification and a Gameful[2] Life[3] in action. But each will be a separate, unique, and multi-dimensional Self-Gamification experience for me to write, with the addition of new

---

[1] Parable: "a simple story told because it represents a basic moral truth or religious principle" — dictionary.cambridge.org/dictionary/english/parable

[2] Gameful: "Playful, sportive; light-hearted; jesting, humorous." — www.lexico.com/en/definition/gameful

[3] Gameful Life: "To lead a more gameful life, you simply have to be open to learning about the psychology of games—and be willing to experiment with new ways of thinking and acting that can help you increase your natural resilience." — Jane McGonigal, *SuperBetter*

or re-designed Self-Motivational Game designs. I am really excited about this.

There are several reasons why *Gameful Project Management* is Book 1 in the "Gameful Life" series.

First of all, through interactions with my readers, I realized that many of them were either entrepreneurs, or persons in management positions. So, their questions were often centered around turning project management into games. Also, besides work, many questions were about how to handle what we want or need to do, balancing it with enough time for our loved ones, our friends, and ourselves.

While answering their questions, I shared my process of turning first parts of my life, and then my whole life, into games. I also shared my Self-Motivational Game designs. At some point, I realized that many of these designs involved project management, both for single projects and for the management of multiple projects, embracing both my work and personal life.

The interest in Self-Gamification resulted in several requests for me to lead seminars and give presentations on the topic. These requests, and questions during the workshops, seemed to again come down to this one question: How can we make juggling the various responsibilities we have, not just productive, but enjoyable too? The possibility of enjoying whatever we are up to, which I show in my approach to turning our lives into games, was one of the main drivers for me to share what I had to say.

And here is another reason, which explains both why this book should be the first in the series, and why the above is true.

We *build* our lives, right from the moment we are born. We might not realize it for a long time, but we do. First, through mimicking others, and later experimenting with our own creativity.

The building blocks of our lives have various dimensions, colors, and structures. We refer to some of these as moments, days, weeks, months, years, or as milestones, toddler-, formative- and other years. Some of them are not so much blocks as they are ribbons running through our lives, for example the sports we love to play, genres we like to read, our hobbies and passions, and of course, our jobs.

And then there are our projects.

They can be as colorful as the other building blocks and ribbons. Some are short; others take years to complete.

The following quote underlines the truth of this:

"Being a Project Manager is like being an artist, you have the different colored process streams combining into a work of art." — Greg Cimmarrusti

We are all artists; all of us are project managers. And at least once in a while, we are also team leaders.

As a result, our lives are ever-evolving products of nature and of human art, and at the same time, they are project (and life) management processes too.

# The Coffee Breaks, One Day at a Time

# Day 1:
# Introduction -
# About This Book

**Reading time: 9 minutes**

Here are answers to questions frequently asked about a non-fiction book.

## 1. Why this book?

Similarly with *Self-Gamification Happiness Formula*, this book was born because I couldn't find any resources on approaching project management as if it was a game, and to address it as such from the perspective of both a game designer *and* a game player.

I found many resources on project management gamification, as well as serious, educational games on project management. I also found books on "playful project management." But a search for the words "gameful project management" didn't return any fruitful results.

Since projects are much closer in structure to games than play, and since games can provide so many inspiring ideas, I felt compelled to write this book.

The other reason is that I mentioned in the previous chapter introducing the "Gameful Life" series. Many questions I get on Self-Gamification are directly related to project management, often how to manage multiple projects at work or home.

## 2. What is this book about?

This book is an awareness booster.

That is what all non-fiction — especially those on personal and business development — and also some fiction books, video courses, documentaries, films, inspiring workshops, seminars, and conferences, as well as meet-ups with peers and friends, are. If we allow it, they can all boost our awareness of what else is possible, in addition to what we already know.

And that is what this book is about. I wrote it to raise your awareness of what is possible when you turn project management into Gameful Project Management; in other words, if you approach your projects, including the management of them, as if they were games, and as if you were both the designer *and* the player of these games.

## 3. What is this book *not* about?

And here is what *Gameful Project Management* is *not* about.

It is not an academic book.

Nor is it an exhaustive resource on the topic of Self-Gamification, which serves as the basis for Gameful Project Management. For an in-depth discourse on the Self-Gamification approach, go to *Self-Gamification Happiness Formula*.

This book is not about you buying new software or hiring new personnel.

We won't be looking for the reasons you don't feel as in control as you'd like over your projects, project management, or life.

This book is not about being too serious or demanding of yourself or your team. There is a word in project management that is often used: "accountable"[4]. I feel it is sometimes used to add drama and exaggerate the need for precise recording of progress on a project, which is not always possible. And as a result, we put too much weight on the person who is expected to be accountable.

---

[4] "Accountable = Someone who is accountable is completely responsible for what they do and must be able to give a satisfactory reason for it." — dictionary.cambridge.org/dictionary/english/accountable

But excellence is not perfection. According to Elizabeth Gilbert, perfection is fear in disguise[5]. Excellence is inherent to the gamers who enjoy the games they play. But there is no drama (or only jokingly expressed upsets) when they play games, while we seem to insist on loading our projects with drama and seriousness. So instead of putting too much weight and drama on project management activities, by claiming that they are vital and critical (which they might be in some situations, and not in others), you will learn how to address them lightly and gamefully, and at the same time with excellence and perseverance. After all, those who have fun with what they do, are successful at what they do.

Project management is about saying both "yes" and "no." But we won't be assigning things as either "good" or "bad." I learned that if I keep things around for a while, then I want to do them, despite giving them all kinds of labels. The gameful approach that I address in this book will help you to put that labeling urge aside, and to view what you do as games instead.

The *Gameful Project Management* book is not about overthrowing the practices developed by the masters of project management. I was amazed to discover that project management knowledge has been collected worldwide for over 250 years[6]. No,

---

[5] www.youtube.com/watch?v=NlLyeozPmOs

this book is not about replacing all this knowledge with a new approach, or distilling it in any way. It is about supplementing the essential project management toolkit.

## 4. Who is this book for?

This book is for everyone interested in making project management not only productive and effortless, but also fun.

## 5. What will you learn in this book?

You will learn about the synergy of anthropology (= awareness), kaizen (= small steps) and gamification (= bringing fun game elements into what we do). These three approaches are brought together by Self-Gamification, and when it comes to project management, by Gameful Project Management.

Here is why.

Without being aware of and appreciating what you have already achieved or what you have at your disposal, you won't be able to grow. You need to know your "soil," the "grains" and the

---

[6] From the introduction of the book *Managing Yourself* by Elizabeth Harrin: "It's over 250 years of project management experience distilled into 241 pages so you can see how other people run their projects outside the management texts and research papers: how projects get done in the real world."

"weather/landscape" conditions at this moment (not some future point), to identify the best next step to achieve the result you would like.

Without being willing to take a small step at a time, and to make only a little or no investment for each of these small steps, you won't be able to grow continually. Instead, you will experience bumps.

Without adding a fun factor to what you do, without enjoying what you do, you will struggle to produce something that others will enjoy too.

By introducing these three skill sets, the book will equip you with simple tools to address any challenges you experience with your projects, and the management of them.

You will learn how to improve performance in your project management without considerable investments in expensive technology or new personnel.

You will find out how to achieve these improvements using what you already have at your disposal, and with minimal additional effort.

You might also experience what I did, when time and money were saved in a project — that the company I worked for as a sub-contractor received referrals, not only from their customer, but also from their customer's client. The most fantastic thing about this achievement is that the only parameter changed was the gameful approach described in this book.

You will also discover that saving time and money comes as a natural result, as does the acquisition of new customers. These are the by-products of embracing the essence of Self-Gamification and Gameful Project Management.

For you, as the project manager, this essence is to approach each project and project management *with awareness, in small steps, and gamefully.*

## 6. What do you need to know or do before reading this book?

There are no specific requirements before reading this book.

You don't need to read *Self-Gamification Happiness Formula,* which addresses Self-Gamification in detail, and on which this book is based.

However, you are, of course, welcome to read it if you wish to find out more about how you can consistently turn any project or activity into fun games.

But if you'd like to read this book, for now, read on.

## 7. How to read this book?

Many of us have been asked, "Try to explain that in such a way that you could fit the whole concept on a napkin."

I love words and "painting" pictures with words, so I thought, "How could I explain what I have to say without even a napkin and pen available?"

The following scenario came to mind.

Imagine you and I work at the same company, but in different departments. One of us is relatively new to the company, so we don't know that much about each other. Or we are two entrepreneurs who work every day in the same library or cafe. And lately we happen to have a coffee break together.

One day you find out about this quirky approach I have of turning any project or activity in my life (and even sleep at night) into fun games, and that I reward myself with points, badges, and stars. You have also heard how I saved the company money and got new customers through this gameful attitude. So you want to know more.

For the next month, you ask me to devote our coffee break to sharing this approach with you.

Each month has, on average, twenty-one full workdays. Almost accidentally, this book contains twenty-one chapters, which I call "days" (including this chapter here).

Each chapter can be read in ten minutes or less. I have estimated the reading time at the start of each chapter, based on the average reading speed of 200 words a minute[7].

I have put the following line at the end of each chapter ("day"): "Your gameful epiphanies for today:", to give you the space — both mentally and on the page (if you are reading a paperback) — to become aware of your own discoveries, inspired by the text of this book. Each of us might read the same text but be inspired in different ways. And these ways might even differ for the same person in different circumstances.

You are welcome to read the book at your own pace or in the sequence you like. Each of the chapters, or "days," has — in addition to a number — a title, to give you a hint of what it is about.

I hope that each of the chapters (our "daily coffee-breaks") will give you an insight into how you can enrich whatever you do, including your project management activities, into fun, rewarding, successful games, and provide inspiration that culminates in your own epiphanies as the designer and player of these games.

A side-note: I have capitalized the words in four phrases throughout this book, although they

---

[7] www.irisreading.com/what-is-the-average-reading-speed/

are not yet trademarks. These are: Gameful Project Management, Fun Detecting Antenna, Self-Gamification, and Self-Motivational Games. I have done so because the use of these is currently unique — to the best of my knowledge — to the motivational books I have written. I have also capitalized the phrase "Gameful Life" a couple of times (primarily when referring to this book series), but not throughout the book, since it is not exclusive to this series or my other books, and has been used many times elsewhere.

# Your gameful epiphanies for today:

# Day 2:
# What are My Qualifications?

**Reading time: 5 minutes**

When we teach or share something, we often contemplate and report on our experience with the subject at hand.

I might have been the first person to use and define the terms "Gameful Project Management," "Self-Gamification," and "Self-Motivational Games", but it isn't the sole reason I believe I am qualified to talk about turning project management (or anything else) into fun games.

Let's consider my experience with game-related topics and project management, in turn.

Why am I qualified to teach on the topic of turning things into games?

I first consciously turned something into a game six years ago, before I had heard the word gamification, and before I started to read books on game design[8] and game thinking[9]. My "serious"

---

[8] Game design: "The art of applying design and aesthetics to create a game for entertainment or for

interest in games, game design, and gamification came three years later.

I am a non-gamer without any specific qualifications in software, game, or gamification design, nor in psychology. I may well be one of the first persons of this kind to explore gamification and apply it to themselves. And to teach it.

My lack of a game-design background is, in fact, an advantage. Because, if *I* can turn my projects and life into fun games without having studied gamification or psychology in detail, then so can you.

I believe my primary qualification for explaining and teaching Gameful Project Management and Self-Gamification is the enormous fun I have had turning my life into games; experiencing happiness multiple times every day while doing so; and never wishing to stop designing and playing my self-motivational and uplifting games.

---

educational, exercise, or experimental purposes. Increasingly, elements and principles of game design are also applied to other interactions, in the form of gamification." — en.wikipedia.org/wiki/Game_design

[9] A great example of resources on how to facilitate and achieve game thinking is *Game Thinking*, by Amy Jo Kim

My experience with project and team management has already spanned several decades.

My first experience with project and team management was in my school years, in the former Moldovan Soviet Socialistic Republic. It started with managing sewing projects for younger girls and helping them sew items for their dolls. I organized our meetings and made sure I had extra material and tools with me. I also taught them how to do it. My skills were quite elementary, so I often needed a "consultant." My mom happily took on this role.

I was also the head of the Oktiabrionok[10], Young Pioneer[11], and Komsomol[12] groups, first in my class, and later for the whole school.

---

[10] Oktiabrionok: "октябрёнок oktiabrionok (child between the ages of seven and eleven, in the first stages of Communist training)." — en.wikisource.org/wiki/Page:Dictionary_of_spoken_Russian_(1945).djvu/397

[11] Young pioneers: "a mass youth organization of the Soviet Union for children of age 9–15 that existed between 1922 and 1991. Similar to the Scouting organizations of the Western world, Pioneers learned skills of social cooperation and attended publicly funded summer camps." — en.wikipedia.org/wiki/Vladimir_Lenin_All-Union_Pioneer_Organization

[12] Komsomol: "a political youth organization in the

I don't remember leading any teams during my university years, but there were many projects to take care of, both at home and for my studies.

After several years of work as a researcher at the Institute of High-Frequency Electronics of the Technical University Darmstadt, I was appointed as the coordinator of our laboratory and its clean-room.

Since then I have led small and large teams, both within a single organization and the global working group of an international community (the latter for almost twelve years).

The projects I managed or helped to manage varied from small, through medium, to large, both for the private sector and for such organizations as ESA, NATO, and German and other Defence organizations.

Today I manage various projects at home and for my business. The teams for these projects include my family, and the entrepreneurs who help me with my book and online course projects,

---

Soviet Union. It is sometimes described as the youth division of the Communist Party of the Soviet Union (CPSU), although it was officially independent and referred to as 'the helper and the reserve of the CPSU'." — en.wikipedia.org/wiki/Komsomol

including navigating the world of marketing and publicity.

Despite such varied and extensive experience with project and team management, I am still an unofficial project manager[13], never having received formal training in the area.

The closest (but still quite remote) thing to such formal training was a summer camp with training courses for schoolchildren who volunteered as heads of their Komsomol school committees in Moldova, during the Perestroika years in the former Soviet Union. It is fun to recall those times now. I must say that, among other things, I learned many soft-skills there that still apply, and today are taught all over the world.

Apart from that, I have participated in training courses on disciplines and tools that are related to project and organizational management. Examples are SAP[14] and S1000D[15].

---

[13] Unofficial Project Manager: "If most of your work time is spent on projects and you've never been exposed to formal project management training, you are an unofficial project manager." — Kory Kogon, Suzette Blakemore, James Wood, *Project Management for the Unofficial Project Manager*

[14] SAP: www.sap.com

[15] S1000D: www.s1000d.org

I have also taught numerous S1000D training courses, including the topic of Business Rules, which are the knowledge base of all decisions (many hundreds of them) on how to implement this international specification for technical publications.

I also lead various teams in addition to the Business Rules Working Group (BRWG) of the S1000D community (for almost twelve years, as already mentioned above), of which I am still a member. BRWG is responsible for developing concepts for S1000D implementation and S1000D project management.

I have devoted several books to business rules, both for those who implement S1000D and project managers and entrepreneurs in other areas, to help them gain control of their decision making, be it in S1000D or anything else.

Now, as I write a book that deals with project management, I reach out to my current favorite teachers — books (and sometimes articles) — to learn more about this multi-dimensional discipline.

I have read books on project and time management in the past, but only now that I've been turning my life into fun games for several years have I become aware of something in most of the resources on project management, which I hadn't noticed before. I will share it with you later in the book.

But before that, let's consider why it makes sense to turn projects and project management into fun games.

# Your gameful epiphanies for today:

# Day 3:
# Why Turn Project Management Into Games?

**Reading time: 7 minutes**

Let's look at the reasons why it makes sense to turn project management, among everything else, into fun games.

The order below feels right to me right now (note: it's not hierarchical), but you are free to read these reasons in the order that feels most appropriate to you. Each paragraph is a reason. I numbered these reasons for your convenience.

Please note that this list is not exhaustive. Use the space at the end of the chapter to add your own reasons why Gameful Project Management makes sense.

1.  Projects are the building blocks of our professional and personal lives. So, to live joyfully, we also need a joyful approach to our projects.

2.  Drama falls away in games. If we look at what we want or have to do as a game, then the

stakes are not that high, are they? It's just a game, isn't it?

3. We are less reluctant to start playing a game than we are to say "yes" to a real-life project.

4. We are less critical of ourselves in games. In a computer game we don't dwell on the fact that we just bumped our car into a wall. Instead, we notice what happened, reverse, turn the car around, and move on. We can do the same in our real-life "games" (including projects and project management activities).

5. We are less afraid of failure in games. In fact, failures in games are often not considered as such, but as steps on the way to winning. Which is especially true for game design. Discarded game designs are rarely regarded as failures. They are scarcely analyzed for why they "failed" at all. They are just steps on the natural progression towards the successful design.

6. When you see and treat whatever you are up to as a game, you can better deal with fear and anxiety. Self-Gamification and its three components can help you to address and bypass fear and anxiety, which are as present in project management as any other activity in which we want to succeed. The more we want to succeed, the bigger the fear, of both failing

and succeeding, as well as what people might say in either of these scenarios. But if what we do is just a game, then the fear diminishes considerably, and we are more willing to try again or try something new.

7.  In games, you don't stay upset for too long. If you do, then you stop playing the game. To continue playing, you need to put your upset aside and focus your attention on the next move in the game. Or to another game. Imagine how much easier real-life projects can become if you proceed with them in the same way. In real-life projects, you can do the same: acknowledge the upset and move on.

8.  When you no longer spend so much time on upsets and complaints, you save an enormous amount of time. I observed this consistently in many projects I turned into games. What happens then is that the projects or tasks are completed with much less effort than anticipated, and often before the deadline (or at least on time). So you also save money in the process. And thanks to the great atmosphere in the project, and better results than expected, you might even get referrals, not only from your customer, but from your customer's customers too — all as a result of awareness, small steps, and gamefulness.

9.  When we see and treat our projects like games (which we both design and play), then we can stop seeing the challenges the project poses as a hardship, but rather as something fun, to be addressed with curiosity and creativity.

10. You might even become curious about something you previously resented. You might find you are suddenly eager to start work on the project now, just like you couldn't wait to try out a new (or old but newly rediscovered) toy or game when you were younger.

11. It is much easier to be present and give our best in games. If we enjoy a game we don't try to get it over with. And if we don't have fun playing it, we either leave it for another game (or something else), or modify the design so that we do enjoy it.

12. As a game designer, you feel in control; you can be that in project management too. Because as the designer of your projects and project management games, you can adjust one or both of the following: the way you approach them, and the way you record your progress.

13. Game designers are utterly resourceful. And you can be that too, in an instant, if you become aware that you are both the designer (or co-designer) *and* player (co-player) of your project games. If you consider anything you do as a

game, of which you are the designer and the player, then you immediately become resourceful on how to adjust the flow of your work so that it becomes fun for you and all involved. With gameful practice, resourcefulness becomes effortless and extremely fun.

14. Empathy is more natural in games, and we judge our partners in games less than partners and customers in projects.

15. Turning your life into games allows you to treat yourself as your best (customer) player and at the same time, your favorite game designer, to whom you gladly give your feedback to make your favorite games even better. And when you treat yourself like that, you will also treat others with kindness more consistently, and vice versa, since people tend to mirror our behavior toward them.

16. In games, we don't resent having to record or document our progress: in fact, we love it. Because, with each move of our figurine on a leaderboard, we get closer to winning the game. If you despise writing reports or creating and updating checklists, project (or business) plans, road-maps, and others, then seeing them as your project game feedback system can help. And then modifying these in a fun and creative

way will help you put your resentment aside with almost no effort.

17. Gameful Project Management enables low-budget, effortless, enlightening, and fun optimization of all facets of your project management. You might frown at this sentence, but this is precisely how the management of your projects and your time can become when you turn them into exciting games and treat yourself as if you were both the designer *and* the player of your project management games.

18. Turning project management into games will not require you to buy a new software system or hire new personnel. Instead, you can concentrate on improving your project management activities with what you already have at your disposal, and with little additional effort. With a self-gamified attitude to project management, you will become aware of what you need for your work (and even life in general) and make conscious decisions on what to do next. You will also acquire gameful resourcefulness and motivation in any situation, including tight deadlines when increased motivation is hard to achieve but often needed.

19. Games and game design are an endless well of creative solutions for project management. "The

design and production of games involves aspects of cognitive psychology, computer science, environmental design, and storytelling, just to name a few. To really understand what games are, you need to see them from all these points of view." — Will Wright in the foreword to *Theory of Fun for Game Design* by Raph Koster. So why not tap into such a multidimensional and fun discipline for inspiration?

20. Since games are fun and contain elements that contribute to our happiness, why not approach all our projects and activities in such a way that they become fun, engaging, and entertaining for us, in the same way that games do? If we use *fun* as the goal, compass, and measuring tool in our projects, along with awareness and progress in small steps, then quality, excellence, success, improvement, productivity, efficiency, and all the other criteria of a successful project and business will come naturally as by-products.

21. Any project is already a game; we just don't always see them that way.

## Your gameful epiphanies for today:

# Day 4:
# What Projects Should Be Turned into Games?

**Reading time: 7 minutes**

You can turn any project or activity into a game — both at work and at home.

But there is another aspect to what we can or *should* gamify (turn into games). I discovered that most satisfaction comes when I turn those tasks into games that appear tricky or tough. A task seems tough and overwhelming when I resist it. Turning those tough tasks into enjoyable and fun activities helps me melt my procrastination and increase my desire to "play" them. That is the actual fun of Self-Gamification.

Let's look into this a little more.

Many of us have learned at various points in our lives to classify our projects and tasks into urgent and non-urgent, important and unimportant. I learned and tried to apply this system multiple times too.

While turning my life into games, and by observing myself and the world around me non-judgmentally, I discovered that there are only two types of projects and tasks depending on how I treat them.

I either:

- escape from them, or
- escape to them.

That is it. Nothing more.

There is, of course, psychological research about how and why we behave in various situations. Human behavior is so complex that there are numerous scientific disciplines studying and trying to explain it.

Thus, it is even more amazing to realize that, independent of the causes for our actions, we treat whatever we want or have to do in only two ways:

- We either avoid them (in other words, we don't do them), or
- Do them while escaping from other things.

## Escape-from tasks

What are the tasks and projects from which we tend to escape — those we procrastinate about before attending to, or avoid forever? What are these?

When I considered what these were for me, I realized that there were again two types, or sub-types, of projects and tasks, independent of whether they had to do with work, my family and friends, or myself.

My thought processes determined these two sub-types of escape-from tasks, and this is how I thought of them:

- *Sub-type 1:* I either felt that I wanted to do them very much, but didn't have time for them, or
- *Sub-type 2:* I thought I didn't want to do them but had to do them.

Here are some examples of the tasks I wanted to do but thought that I didn't have time for (sub-type 1):

- I wanted to spend more time writing my works-in-progress during the day but I couldn't because I had so many other things to do.
- I wanted to learn and speak better Danish (since I live in Denmark).

Here are examples of the tasks I needed to do because I had committed to them, but claimed or thought that I didn't want to do them (sub-type 2):

- I didn't like doing bookkeeping for my business, but I had to.
- I didn't like working out or doing any kinds of sports, but I had to because it was better for my health.

While practicing Self-Gamification, I discovered something surprising that now sounds logical and revealing to me. The tasks we "have" to do must also be something we "want" to do. Otherwise, we wouldn't keep them around, but would give them up entirely after some time. We can become aware of this by recognizing that they are, in fact, parts of the more significant projects or goals we want to achieve. Such as preparing for exams to get the degree we want.

**Escape-to tasks**
Now, let's consider the things that we escape to. The things that we choose to do before those discussed in the previous section. Let's take a look at the projects and tasks we blame for our procrastination of escape-from tasks.

I discovered that here, there are also two sub-types. There are "obvious" and "productive" escape-to tasks.

The obvious are those we describe as, "I deserve a break, so I'll do that instead of what I planned to do."

These could be, for example, watching TV or random videos on YouTube, reading a book for leisure, playing an online game, staying in bed, spending time on social media, surfing the internet, etc.

And the second type is productive activities, but not necessarily those that are urgent or necessary to reach our set goals. Instead, these are beneficial but non-urgent, and things we might attend to when we "should" be doing other more pressing activities or those we claim we want to do.

For me, that used to be doing laundry (or in the absence of it, other household chores). If I was finding it a challenge to write an article or a blog post or a book chapter or to compile advertising copy for my books and services, I sometimes followed the impulse to go and check if there were enough dirty clothes to wash or any clean and dry laundry to fold.

Others might choose, for example, gardening before any other things they have to do. Or, if you work in an office, you might find yourself re-structuring the folders on your shelves (or in your computer file system) or some similarly useful but not necessarily urgent activity.

**Escape-from and escape-to tasks can switch places**
While reading (or listening to) the above, you might have found it difficult to differentiate clearly between escape-from and escape-to activities, when thinking of your own.

This could be because the activities we escape from can become those we escape to, and vice versa, depending on our state of mind.

The first time I noticed this myself was when I was putting off laundry, but checking the accounts for my business almost daily. There were rarely income and expense entries every day for my one-person business, but I let the laundry grow into a considerable mountain nonetheless.

## How can this classification help you?

You might have felt a little uncomfortable looking at what you escape from and escape to, and at the complexity of your thought processes. So why do it?

The purpose is to give you a simple approach by which to study your behavior toward various projects and activities, as well as your thought processes, anthropologically — in other words, non-judgmentally.

This will make you aware that you procrastinate about not only the things you think you don't want to do but have to, but also the projects you believe you cherish.

Awareness of your escape-from and escape-to projects and activities, in various situations and states of mind, can help you design your Self-Motivational Games in such a way as to create an enticing challenge. Beyond that, you can give yourself more rewards for your escape-from projects and activities, and limit the rewards for escape-to activities.

For example, I limited points to a maximum of one per day for doing laundry. If I gained a point for it on a particular day, doing more laundry wouldn't earn me any more points. This motivated me to return to writing, and the other activities I feared and procrastinated about, as I could gain more points for those instead. Giving myself a point for each tiny bit of a task I procrastinated about, for example, for writing a paragraph of my book or working for a few minutes on another escape-from project, made those tasks more attractive and effortless to accomplish.

If an escape-to task switched places with an escape-from task, then I adjusted my Self-Motivational Game accordingly, for example, when laundry and bookkeeping switched places. I reserved a spot on my calendar for each Friday to check my business and private accounts, and update my business books and personal expenses. Until Friday came, I wouldn't get any checkmark (or point) for doing this task. Now I was free to do the other tasks I had on my to-do list, like laundry, for example, which had become an escape-from task.

# Your gameful epiphanies for today:

# Day 5:
# When Should Projects Be Turned into Games?

**Reading time: 2 minutes**

The answer to this is similar to the previous question, "What Projects Should Be Turned into Games?" There, I answered, "Anything."

And here, the answer is, "Any time. Especially any time you need help."

You see, when you are in the flow[16], your work is progressing well, and you are enjoying what you are doing, then you don't need help. You simply have fun with whatever you do. So, don't stop the flow when you are in it.

---

[16] Flow: "There is virtually nothing as engaging as this state of working at the very limits of your ability — or what both game designers and psychologists call 'flow.' When you are in a state of flow, you want to stay there: both quitting and winning are equally unsatisfying outcomes." — Jane McGonigal, *Reality is Broken*

But if there is no flow — and that happens every once in a while — and if you have stepped off your happy, productive path and feel lost, then you can use the tools described here to help you. Self-Gamification (and thus also Gameful Project Management) and the three approaches it embraces, helps you to return to the flow.

So, when you observe that the project is stalling, and you are continually forcing yourself to move in leaps (especially mental ones) that you can't really achieve (and are suffering because of it), then stop.

Next, be your own anthropologist, by observing the situation you are in, your state of mind, and what there is to be done.

Then, as a designer, adjust your game-design so that you, as a player, enjoy your project game.

And finally, as an avid player, identify your next, small and effortless, step in the game and take it.

To maintain balance, you need to move one small step at a time. That applies both to our physical state (when we're awake) and our mental one.

**Your gameful epiphanies for today:**

# Day 6:
# By Whom and Where Should Project Management Be Turned into Games?

**Reading time: 4 minutes**

You might wonder why I consider the questions "Who?" and "Where?" in the same chapter.

The reason is in the answers to these two questions, when applied to turning projects and project management into games.

Here are these two questions and the answers to them.

**Who should be responsible for turning projects and project management into games?**
The answer is, "You."

Here is why. If you lead a team and you want to approach the teamwork and projects gamefully, and help your peers to do the same, you need to start with yourself. You are ultimately both the co-player and the co-designer of these games.

You can't motivate others without being motivated yourself. The same applies to successful management, leadership, awareness, living in the moment, anthropological (non-judgmental) seeing, kaizen, and gamification. You might be a gamification designer (and think that you are intrinsically motivated), but if you take everything too seriously instead of approaching it with lightness and gamefulness, then you will have enormous challenges in demonstrating the benefits of gamification to others.

I am not the first to say that starting with yourself is vital. Here is just one of the inspiring quotes I found about project management:

"It is a project manager's job to organise everyone else, and you will be much more efficient at doing that if you can keep on top of your own activities. If you are clear about what you have to do next it will make it easier for you to organise other people and the work of your team." — Elizabeth Harrin, *Managing Yourself*

So, if you think it is worth turning project management into games, the person most qualified to do that for the projects that you manage, is you.

## Where should Gameful Project Management take place?

You could also read this question as, "Where should the turning of project management into games occur?"

The answer to this is why I posed both questions together.

Here goes.

The only place to turn anything into a fun game is where *you* are. I.e., when we are working or doing anything else, *we* are playing that project or activity game. And the game takes place where the player is. It is where each of us is.

This also means that turning the work of others in a project into a game can only be done where *they* are, and *by* them. You can't do it for them.

So don't judge others; they are their perfect designers and players too.

Sometimes, when we have success in our life, we might be tempted to judge others who complain about theirs. But remember that you can't design their games, because your "shoes" won't necessarily fit them. Only they can develop their own Self-Motivational Games, and create their own experiences.

And also remember that when you judge others, you are complaining too. (I had to chuckle when I observed myself complaining about other people's as well as my own complaints, for the first time.) And when you are complaining, you aren't playing your games. So instead of analyzing what others do or don't do while turning (or not turning) their projects and lives into games, concentrate on playing your games and having fun with them. This is the best way to share Self-Gamification and Gameful Project Management.

One more thing.

If your starting point — where you are right now — is upset, then this is the only place you can be. But it is just a starting point. No more, no less.

Let me remind you here of the gift that anthropology, kaizen, and gamification bring together. Being upset is not wrong.

Such "'stress symptoms' … are not signs of disease. They are our body's gift to us to let us know something important is happening that requires our immediate attention. Without these symptoms we would have perished as a species long ago." — Robert Maurer, *Mastering Fear*

We often fail to appreciate these gifts because they don't fit our preferences for the moments in our lives. It is up to us to decide which moments we extend and which we keep short. Each moment is a starting point, after all.

So the next two steps, when your starting point is upset, could be:

1.  Stop and take a non-judgmental look at where you are and what you might be afraid of.

2. In the next moment, after you've had a good look at where you are and the fears you are resisting, do whatever you choose to next in your game. In other words, the next step is entirely up to you.

**Your gameful epiphanies for today:**

# Day 7:
# How Should Projects Be Turned into Games?

**Reading time: 3 minutes**

So far, we have considered all the five W-questions — why, what, when, who, and where.

The remaining question is *how* to turn a project and its management into games.

The answer is multi-faceted, and in a way, the remaining chapters (days) all deal with its various aspects.

The long-term "how" is in the cultivation part of turning projects into games, because as you might have guessed, this is not a one time pill. It is about developing a lifestyle for yourself, and a particular culture in your project environment, both at home and work.

But here is a "short-term" or a "small-step" answer, or, in other words, ideas for the next small steps to take.

When you design your Self-Motivational Games (= your projects or activities turned into games), then if, for example, you measure your score in points, you could do the following.

You can give yourself more points for escape-from tasks; at least one point for each tiny step you take. When you are in the flow, you can let the points be and simply enjoy the project.

For your escape-to tasks and projects, you limit the points. But still praise yourself in some way for attending to them, because they can serve as a recharging break from the intensive games defined by your escape-from projects.

Turning your projects into games and limiting the rewards you give yourself for the "escape-to" activities and increasing the rewards (points, stars, etc.) for your "escape-from" projects will harness your creativity in the direction of your goals and will increase your productivity toward what you want and need to do.

You can also create a Role-Playing Game[17] around it. There are no limits in fantasy.

---

[17] Role-Playing Game: "A role-playing game (sometimes spelled roleplaying game; abbreviated RPG) is a game in which players assume the roles of characters in a fictional setting. Players take responsibility for acting out these roles within a narrative, either through literal acting, or through a process of structured decision-making regarding character development. Actions taken within many

Get inspired by games or anything else that awakens your curiosity.

You don't have to dissect games to get inspired. Whatever spikes your interest or catches your attention, however simple it is, is worth looking at. Timers, background music, countdowns, performing a task in an unusual place (like reading a text-book or article you need to read under a table), each of these and many more can add a fun challenge. The life-changing #5SecondRule by Mel Robbins was inspired by a commercial showing a rocket launch with "the famous final five-second countdown, 5- 4- 3- 2- 1." — Mel Robbins, *The 5 Second Rule*

The "how" in Gameful Project Management is not about trying to drastically change, improve, or force anything in your current practice. You don't need to aspire to change; you will do so anyway, without intending to. But being aware of where and how you are, where you want to head, then moving forward one step at a time in that direction, and finally appreciating each step on the way, can make your life more and more rewarding, and your project more and more exciting and successful.

---

games succeed or fail according to a formal system of rules and guidelines." — en.wikipedia.org/wiki/Role-playing_game

**Your gameful epiphanies for today:**

# Day 8:
# Gameful Project Management and the Synergy of Three

## Reading time: 3 minutes

Often, the name of a concept does not give away everything about it. This applies to Gameful Project Management. As with gamification itself, it is much more than just adding "points, badges, and leaderboards"[18] to your operational processes and reporting systems.

### Self-Gamification as a source

While writing this book for project managers, I lean on the approach I call Self-Gamification, which is

---

[18] One of the most prominent authorities in gamification, with whom I have had the honor of talking online, Yu-kai Chou, often emphasizes — including in the sub-title of his acclaimed book — that gamification is "beyond points, badges, and leaderboards." — Yu-kai Chou, *Actionable Gamification*

the art of turning any- and everything in our lives into games.

The Self-Gamification approach embraces three well-established and known techniques and methods, which can also be described as philosophies.

These are:

- Anthropology,
- Kaizen, and
- Gamification.

Gameful Project Management also has roots in these three approaches.

## Three approaches embraced by Self-Gamification and Gameful Project Management

*Anthropology*[19], as it stands today, is about the non-judgmental study of cultures. And the same can be done on a personal level. You can study yourself as a culture of one person; you. "Practice your anthropological approach. Pretend you're a scientist observing a culture of one — yourself. The trick is not to judge what you see, but to neutrally observe how you function, including your thought processes. Awareness and kindness are key." —

---

[19] Anthropology is "the scientific study of the origin, the behavior, and the physical, social, and cultural development of humans." — www.thefreedictionary.com/anthropology

Ariel and Shya Kane, *How to Have A Match Made in Heaven*

*Kaizen*[20] embraces breaking anything into small, effortlessly manageable bits. This might be a challenge, the path to reach our goals, or even rewards we give ourselves or others for making those small steps[21]. You might also have heard of or

---

[20] Kaizen: "Kaizen (改善) is the Japanese word for 'improvement.' In business, kaizen refers to activities that continuously improve all functions and involve all employees from the CEO to the assembly line workers. It also applies to processes, such as purchasing and logistics, that cross organizational boundaries into the supply chain. It has been applied in healthcare, psychotherapy, life-coaching, government, and banking. By improving standardized programmes and processes, kaizen aims to eliminate waste. Kaizen was first practiced in Japanese businesses after World War II, influenced in part by American business and quality-management teachers, and most notably as part of The Toyota Way. It has since spread throughout the world and has been applied to environments outside business and productivity."
    en.wikipedia.org/wiki/Kaizen

[21] The two brilliant references here are Robert Maurer's *One Small Step Can Change Your Life*, and *The Spirit of Kaizen*

applied the techniques of lean management, which are closely related to kaizen and even referred to as its component. "In the United States, kaizen lives today through practices that include lean production, just-in-time (JIT) delivery, and statistical control of processes." — Robert Maurer, *The Spirit of Kaizen*

Gamification[22] is about bringing the best of what games give us into real-life situations. It is about bringing the fun factor to what we do besides games. It is also about being willing to see what we do in our "regular" lives as games — any project, and any activity.

## Tapping into the synergy of three

In *Self-Gamification Happiness Formula*, I share more on each of these approaches and the work of those I learned about them from.

To keep this book as concise as possible, here is a short summary of why I think these three approaches work so well together. Together, all

---

[22] Gamification is "the use of game design elements in non-game contexts" — Deterding, S., Dixon, D., Khaled, R., & Nacke, L. (2011). From game design elements to gamefulness: defining gamification. In Proceedings of the 15th international academic MindTrek conference: Envisioning future media environments (pp. 9-15). ACM.

three approaches, methods, and philosophies create a fantastic synergy. It has its foundation in awareness, and progresses one brick at a time, to build a beautiful and fun house that we enjoy being in. It is about being both the designers *and* the players of what we do, regardless of whether we think we want, need or have to do it.

So, when in doubt, you re-iterate the following:

1. Become aware of where you are and where you want to head in any given task or project.
2. Identify the next smallest step that you can take with the least effort and resources to move forward.
3. Take and appreciate that step in whatever way you find fun and exciting.

And then, repeat.

**Your gameful epiphanies for today:**

# Day 9:
# Achieving Improvement without Forcing It

## Reading time: 4 minutes

On one occasion when I discussed the book I was writing on Gameful Project Management, and its non-judgmental approach, the person I was talking to asked me what I thought about change management. After a few more minutes' conversation, I understood that by "change," she meant "improvement." So what she was asking was how to adjust project management in order to improve.

### Why is the word "improvement" tricky?
I hear questions about improving what we do or even ourselves a lot recently.

Even kaizen, which is one of the techniques I practice every day, and which is part of the Self-Gamification approach, translates as "continuous improvement." Improvement could therefore be taken as a goal of kaizen.

But I do not experience kaizen as such. If improvement were my goal, then I would be labeling the way I am now — or the status of my projects — as not good enough. But labeling something as bad, or not good enough, is not only stressful and confusing, it is also counterproductive and without meaning.

## What is the best way to improve something?
As it turns out, however strange and paradoxical it may be, the best way to improve anything, including ourselves, is to stop trying to improve it.

That is what Gameful Project Management can do for you. It enables you to achieve improvement without forcing it.

When you approach each of your projects, as well as the project management itself, as if they were fun games — of which you are both the designer and the player — then each moment of your work (and your life) will feel like the best you have had so far. And then, the next will be even better. Improvement will become an effortless by-product; not a forced and impossible goal.

## The anthropological foundation of Gameful Project Management
As discussed in the previous chapter, Gameful Project Management is based on the Self-

Gamification approach, which relies on the synergy of anthropology (= awareness and non-judgmental seeing), kaizen (= breaking everything into small, digestible, and doable bits), and gamification (= bringing fun game elements into what we do).

And the foundation of it all is anthropological, that is non-judgmental, seeing of any of your projects, and the status of them.

Today, anthropologists apply a method they call *"cultural relativism*, an approach that rejects making moral judgments about different kinds of humanity and simply examines each relative to its own unique origins and history."— Cameron M. Smith, *Anthropology For Dummies*

This approach is one of the foundations of anthropology, and it "is the comparative approach, in which cultures aren't compared to one another in terms of which is better than the other but rather in an attempt to understand how and why they differ as well as share commonalities." — Cameron M. Smith, *Anthropology For Dummies*

**What to look at while applying anthropology**
So, next time you think of improving something, or even improving yourself, stop, and look at everything in front of you non-judgmentally. Look at and become aware of:

- Where you are in the project and in general.

- What your circumstances and those in the project(s) are.
- What you have at your disposal right now at this moment.
- Where you want to go with your project(s) — that is, what your goals are in the project.
- Where the customers of your project want you to head with it.
- Where the step you just took directs you — it might be away from the set goals, but don't judge what you see.
- What the various ways are that your brain judges the situation you and your projects are in, and how you judge judgment and complaint, both yours and that of others.
- What is the best next step to take toward your goal — criteria for such a step are: it should be small and effortless to take, and it should be fun.
- How you can appreciate each small step, you take. Remember, it is not about keeping a strict account. (Note: I addressed it in the introduction to this book and will also discuss this further in the book.) It is about appreciation, awareness, and having fun.
- Other things that come to mind as you read this list.

Do all this non-judgmentally, in other words, without labeling something as good or bad and without dramatizing it, but simply iterating from one step to another, discovering the fun in every step of the way, as you usually would in games.

Yes, this is also possible in project management.

**Your gameful epiphanies for today:**

# Day 10:
# Gameful Project Management and Its Focus on Success Instead of Failure

## Reading time: 7 minutes

As I learn more and more about project management, I am struck by how serious most of the resources sound, especially in their introductions. Most of them display statistics of failures and analyze why projects fail.

Having turned many projects and activities (including project management) into games for several years now, I've come to adopt gameful thinking more and more.

A side-note: "gameful thinking" is also referred to as "game thinking." Amy Jo Kim named her acclaimed book *"Game Thinking"*, and in it she describes how to "innovate smarter & drive deep engagement with design techniques from hit games." I have also used the phrase "game thinking" in this book but somehow the word "gameful" resonates more with me. It goes well with such adjectives as "resourceful" and "joyful," and I find myself using the word "gameful" more and more when I refer to "game thinking."

Gameful thinking lets you set the drama, the seriousness about what you have to do, aside, and instead concentrate on excellence and success.

For example, if in a video game, you have a "hard" time managing a level, you do one of the following. You ask a fellow gamer to show you how she or he managed that level. Or you look up a video of that game and level online and watch what others do to finish it.

Then you have an epiphany, addressing the player you just watched in your thoughts or out loud, "Ah, you went to the right side of that pit, and I kept going to the left! That is why the monster ate me, and you finished the level!" (I hope you don't mind an utterly simplified example.)

In real-life projects, when something doesn't work, we search for the guilty party (persons or circumstances) in what we believe happened. And we contemplate all of that before we even think of asking others how they have succeeded in similar situations.

In games, including sports, learning by comparing techniques is very similar to the cultural relativism practiced in modern anthropology, which I mentioned above.

In sports, where you (or your team) perform at the same time as your competitors, such as football, soccer, volleyball, basketball, tennis, badminton, and so on, such a comparative technique is simply achieved by recording the game. You can watch the recording and observe what the other team did to win the ball from you at any particular moment, and how it differed from what you did.

To achieve this in real-life projects might seem more challenging, because you may well perceive yourself (or your team) as performing a task alone, since what others do in a similar situation might not be immediately visible or "recordable."

Here is why a gameful approach to what you do is so helpful.

Once you are in the habit of considering it like, for example, a video game, of which you are both the designer and player, then you won't be stuck in the complaint and despair for long.

Instead, you will think something similar to this, "I wonder what others do in such a situation (level) of this project (game)?"

Game designers often tap into anthropological (= non-judgmentally comparative) techniques, as well as positive psychology, which concentrates on studying success.

Many of the books on game design study success stories. They rarely start with failures. I think this is because they don't consider discarded game designs to be failures, but rather steps on the path to successful ones.

On the other hand, many project management and business resources, and even popular social events, such as "F*ck-Up Nights"[23], start or focus on illustrating failures and their analysis.

The idea behind these is surely very well-meant. The authors and organizers are trying to help those having a hard time to see that they are not alone, and show them how to get out of a problematic "failed" situation.

However, I can't escape the feeling that the illustration of and emphasis on failures, or what we perceive as failure, is as pointless as it would be to analyze why you kept going to the left of the pit instead of right in the previous video game scenario.

Making a choice is as mysterious a process as that of inspiration[24]. Every one of our choices can be supported by countless reasons, as well as countless

---

[23] fuckupnights.com/

[24] Inspiration: "Inspiration is a feeling of enthusiasm you get from someone or something, which gives you new and creative ideas." — www.collinsdictionary.com/dictionary/english/inspiration

ones for not making it, even if we aren't aware of these pro- and contra- reasons at first sight.

Trying to hunt these down and prove them right or wrong is not helpful in any way. You wouldn't do that in a game, or at least not for long. So why do we keep doing it in real life?

Do we do it because proving our point of view to be right is a fun and rewarding process? I'm not so sure. Is it because we fear being either criticized or supported, and then discredited later for what we have done? That is more like it.

But real-life examples show that studying success instead of failure can be empowering as well as life-saving.

One of the Self-Gamification components is kaizen, the philosophy and technique of breaking any challenge, any path to goals, into tiny, easily doable, and digestible bits.

My favorite writer on the topic of kaizen is Dr. Robert Maurer, Director of Behavioral Sciences for the Family Practice Residency Program at Santa Monica, UCLA Medical Center and a faculty member at the UCLA School of Medicine. One of the reasons I enjoy reading his books is his interest in studying success. The title of his website says it all. He called it the "Science of Excellence"[25].

---

[25] www.scienceofexcellence.com/

In his acclaimed book *Mastering Fear*, Robert Maurer shared a story about a book that inspired him to devote his career to the psychology of success. In it, he learned how such deadly diseases as smallpox, malaria, and yellow fever were cured.

He wrote, "Prior to my visit to the library that day, I had assumed, as perhaps you do, that the way we remedy disease is by studying people who are ill and, from there, brilliant researchers in top-notch laboratories develop the miracle drugs needed for a cure. This is not, however, how the majority of these horrible maladies were tamed."

He further reveals that the clue that helped save many lives was not in studying those who were ill, but in "studying those who have stayed healthy in the presence of grave illness and discovering what was different about them." That is anthropology at its best, although it might not have been recognized as such a powerful method yet.

This discovery inspired Robert Maurer "to believe that more significant breakthroughs could be made not by observing those courageously struggling, but by looking at those who were succeeding and discovering what they were doing differently." — Robert Maurer, *Mastering Fear*

And since then he found much confirmation of it.

Gameful Project Management, embracing anthropology, kaizen, and gamification, can help you to stop struggling, and instead cultivate gameful thinking and anthropological study that will bring success to yourself and those around you, be it at work or home.

P.S. Once I got through the failure statistics with as little judgment as possible, I observed myself enjoying the project management books more and more. My guess is that it could be seen as the authors sharing their best practices, and it is utterly fun and inspiring to watch "other players play their games successfully."

**Your gameful epiphanies for today:**

# Day 11:
# Gameful Project Management versus Project Management Gamification

**Reading time: 4 minutes**

When I first embarked on my adventure with Gameful Project Management, I couldn't find many resources on approaching project management gamefully. I was searching for the following combination of words: "gameful project management."

A bit later, still unable to believe that there could be nothing written on it, given how many gamified software solutions for project management there are, I searched for "project management gamification" instead. And sure enough, there were many articles, at least one master thesis, and various books addressing the topic of project management and gamification one way or another.

I started reading eagerly, determined to learn from, and quote as many of the sources as possible.

But the more I read, the more I felt I was moving in the "wrong" direction. A quote by the award-winning authors Ariel and Shya Kane, whom I have quoted previously, came to mind. They once said, "We have come to realize if we are not having fun, we are moving in the wrong direction."

So, I wondered why reading about gamification and project management wasn't exciting and fun for me, despite being very interested in the topic and finding the narration of the authors engaging. Was I perhaps mistaken in thinking that Gameful Project Management and project management gamification were the same thing?

As I continued to read and learn, trying to approach the learning process anthropologically, in other words, non-judgmentally, I came across a gamification definition that gave me a key to the puzzle.

Here is the definition:

Gamification "is simply applying the techniques used in games in non-gaming contexts, in order to increase the involvement in the activities"[26].

The addition of the words "in order to increase the involvement in the activities" to the classical

---

[26] twproject.com/blog/project-management-gamification-using-games-project-management/

definition of gamification[27] opened my eyes to the difference between gamification and a gameful approach to project management.

Here it is. Gamification has the purpose of using game elements to improve one or more parameters in an organizational unit, wherever or whatever it might be.

However, the wish to change or manipulate something into changing (such as to improve something), would be an impediment to turning your projects and project management into fun games. Because you wouldn't simply be playing a game. You would be too "stressed out" trying to achieve your goal. No game elements can make such an activity fun.

When you choose to play a "traditional" game (those you want to play to have fun), you are rarely attempting to improve your current situation or reach a certain outcome in any of your projects or real life.

You just play the game and enjoy it.

---

[27] Gamification is "the use of game design elements in non-game contexts" — Deterding, S., Dixon, D., Khaled, R., & Nacke, L. (2011). From game design elements to gamefulness: defining gamification. In Proceedings of the 15th international academic MindTrek conference: Envisioning future media environments (pp. 9-15). ACM.

It is true that by choosing to play a fun game, you might be looking to improve your mood, but not in order to manipulate the status of your projects (or your life) in any way.

As soon as you start to play the game, or read the instructions, your attention shifts from wanting to improve your mood to the goal and rules of the game in front of you.

Thus, Gameful Project Management is *not* the same as applying the gamification process to project management. It is not about distracting you from work either, although once in a while, having a healthy break can be beneficial.

It is about cultivating the ability to see what you do in your project and project management as a fun game (we will address this later in more detail). You both design *and* play this game. So, Gameful Project Management is about giving you the tools to support yourself in your work and bring the fun factor to your projects, without trying to manipulate its outcome.

I wonder if this approach might be the solution to the current challenges faced by gamification solution designers trying to sell their products and services to their customers. Their customers, and in some cases, the solution designers themselves too, don't always see their work and projects as games. But this ability can help all of us to put the drama we tend to create about projects aside, and instead find inspiration in games, bringing their lightness, fun, and joy to whatever we do.

I know from experience that it is possible and easily achievable.

Here is how. Both providers of gamified solutions, and customers, need to study themselves and each other, as well as their interactions, anthropologically, that is non-judgmentally and with total interest. And while doing so, make progress in small steps. And finally, design and play their project and project management games, while using gamified solutions, serious games, simulations and so on, as elements of their daily fun quests, exciting game gadgets, or feedback systems.

**Your gameful epiphanies for today:**

# Day 12:
# Gameful Project Management versus Serious Games

**Reading time: 4 minutes**

In the previous chapter we discovered that Gameful Project Management, or, a gameful approach to project management, is not the same as project management gamification.

So, if it is not gamification, could Gameful Project Management or its outcome be a serious game, or a collection of serious games?

After some research and contemplation, I realized that no, that wasn't it either.

Here's why.

Serious games are "full games that have been created for reasons other than pure entertainment." — Andrzej Marczewski, *Even Ninja Monkeys Like to Play: Unicorn Edition*

Despite being called "serious," these games can be a lot of fun for their players. My son and his classmates love playing grammar and math games at school, which are a combination of learning grammar, math, and other subjects with a ball game or another fun sport activity.

On a more "serious" note, serious games are also used to bring awareness to the intricacy of such issues as patient care, vaccination, and many others for medical personnel[28], as well as in further areas[29].

So, similarly to gamification, serious games also have the purpose of achieving a specific goal, which is often to educate but not exclusively so. For example, "FoldIt is a popular game that is often cited by gamification folk. It is a puzzle game that sets the player the task of predicting the structure of proteins by folding it. Understanding how proteins fold can help lead to the development of cures for all sorts of diseases, including HIV and even Cancer. Humans are really good at solving puzzles, so much so that in just ten days, gamers had solved one enzymatic structure that scientists had been

---

[28] Focus Games in the UK create board games for these and other areas. Their page has a great collection of case studies for the serious games they develop: focusgames.com/case_studies.html

[29] There are many successful companies that create serious games for various requirements. Many of them are also situated in Denmark (the country I live in). Here are just two of them: www.seriousgames.net/ and cphgamelab.dk/en

trying to unravel for more than a decade." — Andrzej Marczewski, "Differences Between Gamification, Simulations, Serious Games and Games"[30]

Here is a quote showing the similarity between gamification and serious games:

"Serious games and gamification have in common that they both use game design and game elements (Marczewski, 2013) and they both serve a business purpose: increasing employee or customer engagement, improving the learning curve in education...The main difference between gamification and serious games is that gamification is not using gameplay where serious games do. Some of the most well-known examples of serious games are Plantville from Siemens (a serious game focused on educating plant management) and 'Pass It On' from AXA Insurance (a serious game focused on personal financial planning) (Marczewski, 2013; AXA, 2011)"[31].

---

[30] www.gamified.uk/gamification-framework/differences-between-gamification-and-games/ and fold.it/portal/

[31] www.pmi.org/learning/library/gamification-project-management-5949; The references quoted in the article:
Marczewski, A. (2013, March). What's the difference between Gamification and Serious Games?

In contrast to this, the goal of Gameful Project Management is not to increase productivity or motivation or engagement, to educate or facilitate learning. All of these are simply by-products of Gameful Project Management.

The goal of Gameful Project Management is to turn any project, and the management of it, into fun, engaging games, of which you are both the designer and the player. Gameful Project Management assumes that you are open to the possibility of seeing projects and project management tasks (regardless of whether you claim to like them or not) as games. When you see what you do as games and each of its components as a game component, then you quickly realize how to modify those components so that your projects and project management "games" entice the players, in other words, everyone involved in them.

The outcome of Gameful Project Management could be a serious game or a gamified solution, but it doesn't have to be. The main outcome of Gameful Project Management is the ability to see what you do as a game and approach it both as a designer and

Retrieved on 29/08/2013 at www.gamasutra.com/blogs/AndrzejMarczewski/20 130311/188218/
AXA. (2011). Company debuts the game of life…insurance. Press Release 13/09/2011.

the player of it. In other words, it is about taking ownership of how these projects and project management games turn out, especially how fun and engaging they are for you and all involved, as players.

Thus, serious games are "created for reasons other than pure entertainment," even though their players can be entertained and have fun while playing them. Whereas, Gameful Project Management can guide you to make your projects and project management processes *entertaining* and *fun*, regardless of whether you initially preferred doing them or not.

## Your gameful epiphanies for today:

# Day 13:
# Defining
# Gameful Project Management

## Reading time: 5 minutes

So, the approach of gameful thinking is different to both gamification, and the process of creating serious games. It is, in my opinion, a yet-to-be-clearly-defined component of seeing and approaching real-life contexts as if they were games.

Let's name the concepts we discussed in the previous two chapters, and the one upon which Gameful Project Management is based:

- Gamification,
- Serious Games, and
- Self-Gamification.

Please note that this list is incomplete. Game inspired design and simulations also profit from game elements and principles, while games themselves, in their classical meaning (along with play), should also be on the list of things that relate to games. If you would like to find out more about the distinctions between all these concepts, I highly recommend an excellent article by Andrzej Marczewski, where he defines these concepts and considers their differences and commonalities[32].

All the approaches listed above in this chapter, except Self-Gamification and Gameful Project Management, concentrate on modifying, "fixing," and improving certain activities, tasks, or aspects of whatever we do, including project management. They also focus on creating concrete products for others to consume to accomplish those tasks. That means that those techniques inspired by games, except Self-Gamification and Gameful Project Management, don't address the space between the activities they focus upon. These approaches don't embrace the fact that the end-users of those solutions need to take ownership of designing their days and should have the freedom to change between solutions as they wish.

Self-Gamification enables you to turn any- and everything into fun games, in other words, you can turn your whole life into fun games, should you wish. It fills the gap between different activities in your day, including project management at work, home, and in your personal life, and presents itself as a gameful "ether"[33]. And since it requires you to

---

[32] www.gamified.uk/gamification-framework/differences-between-gamification-and-games/

be both the designer and the player of everything you deal with during your day, it gives you full control over your choices and all the tools you need.

Gameful Project Management is Self-Gamification focused on project management aspects. Thus, Gameful Project Management is a way to approach project management with awareness, incrementally, and gamefully, which makes it not only efficient and productive but also entertaining and fun.

---

[33] Ether: "According to ancient and medieval science, aether (Ancient Greek: αἰθήρ, aithér), also spelled æther or ether and also called quintessence, is the material that fills the region of the universe above the terrestrial sphere. The concept of aether was used in several theories to explain several natural phenomena, such as the traveling of light and gravity. In the late 19th century, physicists postulated that aether permeated all throughout space, providing a medium through which light could travel in a vacuum, but evidence for the presence of such a medium was not found in the Michelson–Morley experiment, and this result has been interpreted as meaning that no such luminiferous aether exists." — en.wikipedia.org/wiki/Aether_(classical_element)

Let's formulate now the definitions of the three concepts I came up with while turning various projects, project management, and my whole life into fun games. I will start with Self-Gamification and Self-Motivational Games, and conclude with summarizing the meaning of Gameful Project Management.

Here is how I defined Self-Gamification in the *Self-Gamification Happiness Formula*:

- Self-Gamification is the art of turning our own lives into games.
- It is the application of game design elements to our own lives.
- It is a self-help approach showing us how to be playful and gameful, and bringing anthropology, kaizen, and gamification-based methods together.
- In Self-Gamification, we are both the designers *and* the players of our Self-Motivational Games.
- Self-Gamification is about creating uplifting emotions for ourselves and keeping ourselves "happily entertained"[34] with whatever comes our way in our lives.

---

[34] I found the expression "happily entertained" in the following quote: "Games have no other purpose than to please the humans playing them. Yes, there are often 'objectives' in games, such as killing a dragon or saving the princess. But those are all

And here is the definition of Self-Motivational Games:

- A Self-Motivational Game is a real-life project or activity that you adjust in such a way that it feels like a fun game with which you are eager and happy to engage, both in terms of its design and the playing of it.

Thus, any project, as well as any project management task, can become an engaging and fun Self-Motivational Game. When you approach project management gamefully, both as a designer and a player, you turn it into Gameful Project Management.

All that can sound like a colorful "salad" of definitions, and it is. Games are such an embracing unity of various disciplines and inspirations for other parts of our lives, that sometimes when you turn something into games, you might end up with a serious game or a gamified solution. There is never a clear border between these definitions, and there doesn't have to be, in my opinion, because we all will see the definitions slightly differently. There is another fun article by Andrzej Marczewski on why the definitions of gamification, serious games,

---

excuses to simply keep the player happily entertained inside the system, further engaging them enough to stay committed to the game." — Yu-kai Chou, *Actionable Gamification*

and others are important, and why at the same time, they are not that important[35].

All that being said, I invite you to find your own meaning of Gameful Project Management, by approaching it as the designer and player of it. Don't forget to invite your friends, colleagues, and peers to co-design and play it together with you, since:

"Game design isn't just a technological craft. It's a twenty-first-century way of thinking and leading. And gameplay isn't just a pastime. It's a twenty-first-century way of working together to accomplish real change." — Jane McGonigal, *Reality is Broken*

---

[35] www.gamified.uk/2018/11/14/the-importance-of-definitions-and-why-they-dont-matter/

# Your gameful epiphanies for today:

# Day 14:
# Designers and Players:
# The Main Feature of
# Gameful Project Management

**Reading time: 4 minutes**

Of the four main components of games[36], Self-Gamification emphasizes voluntary participation, which seems to be forgotten sometimes in gamified solutions, and when serious games are developed.

A side-note: We will consider the game components, including voluntary participation, and their counterparts in real-life projects, in later chapters of this book.

When I was exploring and formulating the Self-Gamification approach in the book *Self-Gamification Happiness Formula*, I discovered that the main

---

[36] Game: "What defines a game are the goal, the rules, the feedback system, and voluntary participation. Everything else is an effort to reinforce and enhance these four core components."
— Jane McGonigal, *Reality Is Broken*

feature of turning anything in our lives into fun games is the following: We are both the designers *and* the players of our Self-Motivational Games.

Before reading this book or the *Self-Gamification Happiness Formula*, you might have heard this statement as two separate ones:

- "Be the designer of your life," and
- "Here is how you play the game called life."

But I discovered that you can't separate the two. We are both the designers *and* the players of our daily, weekly, monthly, yearly, and so on games, be it at work, at home, or anywhere else.

This is especially true for project management.

Many brilliant resources on project management emphasize that successful project managers start by managing themselves. We discussed this earlier when we considered who is responsible for turning project management into games, and where it should occur.

But how can we turn project management into games?

We can, for example, learn from other players and designers of self-motivational project management games.

Many gamers and skill learners nowadays learn from videos on YouTube and other media, watching how their fellow players play the games (or musical instruments, for example) they love and succeed at playing.

But designers learn that way too. They play other people's games in the genre they are interested in and eagerly study and absorb each detail for inspiration.

Writers do that too. They learn from their peers and idols by reading books in the genres they write.

Project management game designers have an even better situation. They can learn not only from other project managers in their own or other niches, but they can also learn from the designers of games and toys, and the creators of anything that appears playful or gameful. They can absorb almost everything around them like a sponge, wring out what doesn't apply and keep the bits they find fun, to implement them in their projects and work.

A brilliant quote by the legendary Bruce Lee comes to mind here, "Adapt what is useful, reject what is useless, and add what is specifically your own."

Beyond learning from others, asking the following question of yourself and your team, since project management includes team management[37],

---

[37] "Project management is no longer just about managing a process. It's also about leading people—twenty-first-century people. This is a significant paradigm shift." — Kory Kogon, Suzette

can help to jump-start the undoing of even the tightest knots in your projects:

- *For yourself:* "If my project was a game, and I was its designer (which I am!), how would I approach it so that I, as its player, can't wait to start playing (engaging in it) and enjoy doing so, when I do?"

- *For you and your team members:* "If our project was a game, and we were its designers (which we are!), how would we approach it, so that we, as its players, can't wait to start playing (engaging in it) and enjoy doing so, when we do?"

When you ask yourself and your team this question, remember that no idea that appears is wrong. The main criterium to find out what is appropriate for you and your team is how fun it is for all of you.

In the next chapter, I will address the significance of fun for project management.

---

Blakemore, James Wood, *Project Management for the Unofficial Project Manager*

**Your gameful epiphanies for today:**

# Day 15:
# Fun is Not a Bonus;
# It's a Must for Success

**Reading time: 5 minutes**

We all grew up in cultures that taught us to be serious about life and what we wanted to achieve in it. Otherwise, we wouldn't survive either literally or figuratively, or both.

If we wanted to achieve anything in life, we had to work hard. And to underline this seriousness and determination, we learned to complain and surround whatever we wanted or had to do with drama.

Somehow, the opinion that having fun got in the way of achieving anything in life became established in many human minds.

But interestingly enough, the opposite is true. And thanks to globalization, and the internet increasing connectivity, we have become more and more aware of the fact that having fun does not impede success, but rather leads to it.

This is easiest to see in the entertainment industry. When talking about fun, I love quoting Heidi Klum, a German-American supermodel and television personality, and one of the four judges on America's Got Talent (AGT) between 2013 and early 2019.

After the results show of the AGT 2017 finals, a reporter asked Heidi what advice she would give to the winner, Darcy Lynn, a twelve-year-old ventriloquist. Without hesitating, Heidi answered, "Always to have fun. If you don't have fun, it shows in your performance. That is always the key number one."

But also in other areas, including the most technical and business ones, the experience of fun sets you on the path toward success.

"Fun is an extraordinarily valuable tool to address serious business pursuits like marketing, productivity enhancement, innovation, customer engagement, human resources, and sustainability." — Kevin Werbach and Dan Hunter, *For the Win*

Here is another brilliant thought about fun, which I already quoted earlier, but which is worth remembering every once in a while. It is one of my favorite quotes by my favorite authors on living in the moment, Ariel and Shya Kane[38]: "We have come

---

[38] www.transformationmadeeasy.com

to realize if we are not having fun, we are moving in the wrong direction."

But how to find this "right" direction? What is fun anyway?

Fun is a complex term made up of just three letters.

What is fun for us might not be fun for someone else. What we find fun is not only subjective to various persons but even to the same person in different circumstances. We might enjoy playing a game one day and not so much on another.

But there is a great thing about fun. However difficult it is to define in words (I counted, for example, more than ten definitions of fun in just a few chapters of the acclaimed book *Theory of Fun for Game Design* by Raph Koster[39]), we all know what it feels like for us.

---

[39] Here are just five of the shortest ones:
"Fun is light, energetic, playful and...well...fun." — Will Wright in the foreword
"Fun is all about our brains feeling good — the release of endorphins into our system."
"Fun is the act of mastering a problem mentally."
"Fun is contextual."
"Fun is another word for learning." — Raph Koster, *Theory of Fun for Game Design*

Fun can show in different ways. One time while we have fun and enjoy something we might laugh, and at other times, while fully engaged in a video game or fantasy novel, we might frown and appear quite tense. But we are still having fun!

There is another excellent feature of fun. You can discover it anywhere and in anything. Even in those activities you initially claim not to be fun.

We can discover fun when we give that project or activity a chance, approach it with curiosity and without prejudice, while being open to recognizing the fun factors in there, or we can bring fun elements into the project deliberately. Or all of these together.

How can we do this?

Curiosity and passion can help us here. I call them the siblings of fun in this inspirational trio, one preceding and the other succeeding the birth of fun in each moment. These triplets helped us, humans, to choose and pave previously unfathomable paths.

Here is one of my favorite stories on how curiosity leads to passion and fantastic success:

"I was in the cafeteria and some guy, fooling around, throws a plate in the air. As the plate went up in the air I saw it wobble, and I noticed the red medallion of Cornell on the plate going around. It was pretty obvious to me that the medallion went around faster than the wobbling. I had nothing to do, so I start figuring out the motion of the rotating plate. I discovered that when the angle is very slight, the medallion rotates twice as fast as the wobble rate—two to one. It came out of a complicated equation! I went on to work out equations for wobbles. Then I thought about how the electron orbits start to move in relativity. Then there's the Dirac equation in electrodynamics. And then quantum electrodynamics. And before I knew it... the whole business that I got the Nobel prize for came from that piddling around with the wobbling plate."— Richard P. Feynman, *Surely You're Joking, Mr. Feynman!*

Fun has also led me to initially unexpected but utterly rewarding places. I wouldn't have become an author if I hadn't let myself "taste" writing out of curiosity, and let myself follow what felt healing, rewarding, rejuvenating, but most of all, *fun* for me. I have tried various art forms in my life, including singing, playing guitar, painting, making jewelry, and decorations. But it was writing that turned out to be the best way to express myself.

Through all those experiences, I discovered that *fun equaled wholehearted and rewarding engagement*. And that is precisely what defines successful projects and those involved in them. The latter are wholeheartedly engaged, and experience this engagement as utterly satisfying.

**Your gameful epiphanies for today:**

# Day 16:
# Every Game is a Project;
# Every Project is a Game

**Reading time: 5 minutes**

When beginning to create anything, you start a project.

The same applies to games.

If you want to create a game, you are taking on a project that contains many parts to it, both creative and management matters.

Here is how Thomas Schwarzl introduces his book *Game Project Completed*, which among many others addresses the management aspects of a game project:

"This book deals with the underserved topic of how to finish a game project. Technical and artistic work are just the ingredients of the overall process. What makes them stick together and how to manage specific tasks make up the secret sauce to success."

To create a game and make it a finished product, you will need to follow in one way or another the following processes defined by the Project Management Institute (PMI)[40].

"According to the PMI, there are five 'process groups.' Technically, they're not supposed to be 'steps' or 'phases' in managing the project, but it might be easier to think of them that way. They are the following:

1. Initiate
2. Plan
3. Execute
4. Monitor and Control
5. Close" — Kory Kogon, Suzette Blakemore, James Wood, *Project Management for the Unofficial Project Manager*

If you look at these five processes more closely and recall that here in this book we have the ability and the will to see and approach anything we do as games, you will recognize (or at least be able to imagine) that these processes can be seen as quests in your "game project game" or as separate games on their own.

---

[40] Project Management Institute: "Founded in 1969, the Project Management Institute (PMI) sets standards for the project management profession. It has 454,000 members in 180 countries." — Kory Kogon, Suzette Blakemore, James Wood, *Project Management for the Unofficial Project Manager*

To be able to recognize that projects are games too, we need to take a look at the components of games, and determine whether projects consist of these too.

For me, the most revealing definition of game components was the following:

"What defines a game are the goal, the rules, the feedback system, and voluntary participation. Everything else is an effort to reinforce and enhance these four core components." — Jane McGonigal, *Reality Is Broken*

Before I read this definition, I hadn't been able to see the parallels between my projects and games. I might have used a metaphor like "it's a tough game" or similar, but I rarely considered my everyday projects to be games.

Let's repeat the quote by Jane McGonigal and put the components into bullet points. The primary elements of a game are:

1.  The goal,
2.  The rules,
3.  The feedback system,
4.  Voluntary participation.

I am a business owner, so after reading this, I could immediately see parallels between the projects I was working on for my customers, and games. A contract or an agreement, which my customer and I both sign, contains all four of these components. Each project has a goal, there are specific rules, like how I shall do it and by when. There are reporting and evaluation systems in each contract, which is indeed a feedback system even if the progress is not recorded by getting points or badges. And finally, when my client and I sign the contract and make an agreement, we both demonstrate the free will to participate in that project's "game."

The same applies to job contracts which lead to your job "games," with their goals, rules, feedback system (the regular meetings you most likely have with your boss, before or after which you and your employer provide some kind of evaluation of each other), and both sides demonstrating the voluntary participation by signing the employment contract.

Other activities, like sports to stay in shape, also have all four components. The goal could be to live a healthy life. The rules are then the allocation of time you commit to it; the feedback system might be your step counter or an app where you record your workout results every day. Some people take on thirty, one hundred or another amount of days challenges and have social media as their feedback system. Each post recounting a successful workout session is cheered about by their friends and followers.

Voluntary participation might be challenging to see in such cases when we think we don't want to do sports or to develop other healthy habits. However, if we end up working out or doing yoga without someone forcing us, then that is still voluntary participation.

So any project or activity is already a game. We just rarely see them that way.

Why do we need to see and treat what we do as games? If we don't want to see, call, and embrace what we are up to as games, then we won't be able to "play" them and enjoy them in a similar way to games. Only when you become open to seeing your project as a game, can you identify how you can modify its design to make your "project game" exciting and fun.

I will address the topic of the will to see, learn, design, play, and have fun in projects, as in games, in a later chapter.

**Your gameful epiphanies for today:**

# Day 17:
# Approaching Goals
# Anthropologically

**Reading time: 7 minutes**

"The **goal** is the specific outcome that players will work to achieve. It focuses their attention and continually orients their participation throughout the game. The goal provides players with *a sense of purpose.*" — Jane McGonigal, *Reality Is Broken*

Goals in games often pose a fun challenge. For example, release the prince or princess who is being kept captive, and guarded by hideous underworld dragons.

We rarely consider challenges in real-life projects to be fun, especially in one that's stalling or which doesn't run as expected or preferred.

In addition, the goal is always clear and visible in a game. In a real-life project, we often get lost in complaints and forget why we started doing something in the first place.

There is another curious difference between how we consider — and treat — goals in games and projects.

In multi-player (and other) games, all players voluntarily agree to embrace the goals and the rules and have their score recorded in a feedback system given by the game provider.

A side-note: We will consider rules, feedback systems, and voluntary participation in the following three chapters.

In contrast to this, in real-life projects, we tend to be quite resistant toward goals, rules, and the reports we need to prepare (which are simply the various types of feedback systems in your project). Even if we might occasionally enjoy filling in and formatting the report, we will complain about having to do so out of habit more than anything, and the disgruntled feelings won't be far behind.

Is it wrong that we don't resist games as much as we resist projects, and that we are more willing to be excellent and engaged in games than in real-life projects? No, it's not. I'm not trying to blame us humans for taking our lives seriously. We absorbed this attitude in the cultures we grew up in, and from the generation coming before us, who historically had much more challenging lives, with significantly less opportunity and awareness than we do today. We absorbed these attitudes toward various areas of our lives as much as we absorbed and learned the language and the traditions of the cultures we grew up in.

So why did I compare the two situations above? It was an attempt to apply the cultural relativism practiced in modern anthropology, which I mentioned above a couple of times.

In this chapter, the two cultures I am considering non-judgmentally are "us in games," and "us in real-life projects," before we start turning our projects and project management into games.

As you see above, depending on the circumstances we are in ("games" versus "real-life projects"), we can become a different culture.

In fact, understanding that each of us is a culture of our own, can help us understand why each of us sees the goals (which are supposedly clearly defined in a contract with your customer or employee/employer) through different-colored and patterned lenses.

Where do all these different colors come from?

They might come from the secondary goals behind the real-life projects.

The *primary goals* both in games and projects are defined when you answer the question, "*What do we want or need to achieve* to win this game or to bring this project to a successful (= preferred) closure?"

The answers are often very clear: save the prince or princess, or design and make this product by the specified date, with particular quality criteria and satisfying or even exceeding customer expectations.

The *secondary goal* is defined by the question, "*Why* do we want to do that?"

The word "secondary" doesn't mean here that the goal defined by it is less important than the primary goal. It is just not as immediately visible as the latter.

The secondary goal in games, especially in those we play to make us happy, is to have fun and experience happiness while playing. We often greet games, and specifically new games, with a smile and curiosity and a question, "I wonder what playing it would be like."

It is entirely different to how we greet real-life projects. There we often expect "only" work. And the word "work" frequently leaves a bad taste.

Thus the secondary goals in a real-life project are rarely to have fun. They are often to increase productivity, be better than competitors, improve this or that. Here we come again to the pressure and the will to manipulate our current status into something different.

So, again, what is the difference between goals in games and real-life projects?

The goals in fun games pose an exciting challenge, and they are both kind and honest. They also serve you. Here's how. If you go on the quest of rescuing that prince or princess and throw yourself into the adventure to fight or escape those dragons, you will be excited, maybe even laughing happily along the way, experiencing success with each dragon you avoid or defeat. You feel elated *each* step of the way.

In real-life projects, there is often just one successful moment. It is expected to come at the end of the project, if it is done on time, and in conformance with the previously set criteria. The achievements in-between or with less than expected results are rarely celebrated.

So, how can we make the goals of your project games truly gameful in terms of Self-Gamification?

We need to approach them both honestly and kindly. Our goals also need to be of service to others and ourselves. Much like the often-referred-to "Buddha's teachings on skillful speech; he said that we should speak only when what we have to say is true, kind, and helpful." — Toni Bernhard, *How to Live Well with Chronic Pain and Illness*

Toni Bernhard used these criteria toward both others and herself when managing life with chronic pain and illness, and the many tasks and challenges it brought.

When I say kind, honest, and of service to others and ourselves, I don't mean trying to find out if your goals are realistic. You can reach unimaginable and unplanned goals by starting at quite strange places, like the story of Richard Feynman I quoted above.

By trying to be realistic or practical, you might, in fact, suppress your heart's desires, both for yourself and your peers in the project. That is neither kind nor honest, nor is it helpful.

The advice to keep the goals concrete and measurable is helpful, because it prevents us from jumping ahead of ourselves. But we still might resent those concrete and measurable goals, and think that we don't *want* to achieve them, and that we simply *have* to.

So, what's to be done? The following.

Go to that trio mentioned earlier: the *curiosity-fun-passion* trio.

Ask yourself:

- Are you curious about this project? No? What could make you curious (in case you need to address it because you committed to doing so)?
- What could be fun for you in the challenge that the project already poses? What other fun features, challenges could you add to make it hard to leave?

- What are you passionate about? Is there any connection between that and your project? Volunteer to do those parts of the projects that connect your passion to the project. So if you love using Microsoft Excel, volunteer to maintain project spreadsheets or something similar. That will increase your experience of fun.

You probably can see how you can develop this further. Yes, fun is your compass, and at the same time, the measuring tool of your success.

What I recommend is to always have your, as I call it, Fun Detecting Antenna on. This extraordinary device is nothing more than awareness of whether you are experiencing fun, wherever you are, whatever, and however, you are doing at any given moment of your life.

Then you will be on the right track toward your true goals, those you want to achieve with all your heart, especially the true secondary ones, the ones that determine *why* you are working on that project.

**Your gameful epiphanies for today:**

# Day 18:
# Embracing
# the Project Game Rules

### Reading time: 4 minutes

"The **rules** place limitations on how players can achieve the goal. By removing or limiting the obvious ways of getting to the goal, the rules push players to explore previous uncharted possibility spaces. They *unleash creativity* and *foster strategic thinking*." — Jane McGonigal, *Reality Is Broken*

After quoting the definition of game rules by Jane McGonigal, I have a question for you. Is there a project in your life, either work or personal, that sets ridiculous, in your opinion, requirements, or, in other words, rules?

Most of us have (or used to have) at least one such project.

Let's look at something else from a similar standpoint.

Isn't the rule to hit a small ball with a club over a long distance to fall, hopefully after not too many hits, into a small hole, utterly ridiculous too?

Wouldn't it be more straightforward to take a ball in your hand, march straight over to the hole and drop it in there?

Yes, it would!

And yet, if you are a golfer, you would never choose the straightforward solution and instead will take your club faithfully and play by those, possibly strange, rules.

Here's one of the reasons why:

"An old aphorism about golf calls the game 'a good walk spoiled.' That funny quip underscores a fundamental feature of games: games make no sense, and yet we take them seriously *precisely because* they make no sense. The philosopher Bernard Suits calls that seriousness 'a voluntary attempt to overcome unnecessary obstacles.' Golf is a desirable experience *because* it distorts space and time in order to make the player's experience of a landscape more deliberate. We seek out this deliberateness when we play." — Ian Bogost, *Play Anything*

What other differences are there between the rules in golf or any other game, in its classical meaning, and the rules in real-life projects?

First of all, the rules in projects, have specific goals in mind that are different from just having fun. They serve a specific purpose since they are not always designed for entertainment (although they might, at least indirectly, be meant that way, as is the case in the entertainment industry).

But the most significant difference is not in the goals. It is in our resistance to embrace and follow the rules as if we designed them, and they were our idea all along. Even when we have come up with the project and the rules ourselves, we might blame them for not being what we initially planned or imagined. In contrast to that, in games, we readily embrace the rules, which is often visible because we take on that game's identity. For example, we become passionate golfers.

So, even if we sign the contracts and by doing so claim we are willing to engage in the project or job, we still might internally resist the project's or job's rules, judging them as bad, ridiculous, or impossible to function with.

If a golfer on a course crosses his or her arms in front of them and starts judging the inventor of the rules, the clubs, or balls, he or she has completely stopped playing the game, and having fun.

What choice does such a player have now?

They can either:

- Continue complaining from their standpoint, which most probably will lead them to be left behind by their co-players.
- Make a note (either mentally, on a piece of paper, or in an email to themselves) to check

out other game variants or models of balls and clubs on the market to try instead. Or another game altogether. After making that note, the player engages fully in the game as if it was their idea in the first place.

- Make a note to create a new game variant, or model of a club, a ball, or a completely new golf-inspired game after the match has ended, and then either send the suggestion to one of the golf-equipping/game designing companies or "play" with the materials to create these themselves. After making that note, the player engages fully in the game as if it was their idea in the first place.

We have the same types of choices in our real-life projects.

We can either continue suffering from the limits set by the project's rules, or put our curious, studying, and designing hats on.

We could get more information on what else is possible for our project and project management games.

And we could adjust the rules (and possibly also goals and feedback system) of the project in such a way that it becomes engaging, fun, and thus, provides the best possible outcome.

# Your gameful epiphanies for today:

# Day 19:
# At Least
# Four Feedback Systems in
# Real-Life Project Games

**Reading time: 8 minutes**

I've claimed several times above that the reports we must prepare in any project are feedback systems in our project games.

"The **feedback system** tells players how close they are to achieving the goal. It can take the form of points, levels, a score, or a progress bar. Or, in its most basic form, the feedback system can be as simple as the players' knowledge of an objective outcome: 'The game is over when . . .' Real-time feedback serves as a *promise* to the players that the goal is definitely achievable, and it provides *motivation* to keep playing." — Jane McGonigal, *Reality Is Broken*

In traditional games, there might be one feedback system, especially in board-games. In real-life projects, there are usually many.

I found there are at least four main types for each of us and in relation to each project or to multiple projects we want or have to address.

I started calling each of them a "gamebook." Calling them this helped to change my attitude toward them. I began to enjoy maintaining them, which wasn't the case before then.

Let's take a look at these four types of gamebooks.

*First* of all, there is an "Appointments Gamebook." This is usually a calendar, on paper, or digital, where we record our appointments with other people. How can you consider this type of recording a "gamebook"? In other words, what's the goal of this "Appointments Game"? The goal is to manage all or as many recorded appointments as possible. When you consider it like this, some of the appointments you might resent can become less daunting and appear like steps or levels in your "Keeping Appointments Game," and you might even find yourself longing to take part in such events.

The *second* feedback system is the "To-Do List Gamebook" or simply "To-Do Gamebook." I sometimes also call it "Appointments with Myself Book." You could name a game with such a feedback system, a "Strike-Through Game." The goal is to strike-through or cross out all of the items on the list by the end of the game round. This game round could be a day, a week, a month, a year, or another entity, like a project or a work package. Other versions of such feedback systems are checklists, bucket lists, and so on.

As for the calendar with your appointments, you might find it difficult to see your to-do lists as a game token at first. But if you think of some board or card games, where each move consists of many steps, you might recognize that the sequences of these steps are like entries on a to-do list. That means that you can — if you set your mind to it — see your to-do lists as game plans too. And bring fun into them. You just need to figure out how. It is always worth approaching it in a non-judgmental, one-little-step-at-a-time, and gameful way.

I recently realized that you could compare a to-do list at the start of the day to a hand of cards you've been dealt, where you need to get rid of all the cards to win.

I use a daily calendar for my "To-Do List Gamebook", to spread the tasks I have to do over various days of the week and even over different months. Inspired by an agile project management approach SCRUM[41], I move the tasks from one day

---

[41] SCRUM: "Nowadays Scrum is considered the most adopted agile project management framework around the world.

to another if I see that they are not doable on any particular day.

In the course of designing my to-do lists, I have tried many approaches: writing on scraps of paper, sticky notes, or in a notebook; several online and standalone tools; and even an electronic pocket organizer. I discovered that each time I found a method, and it seemed to work, I hoped that it would work forever. I became aware that I was putting too much pressure on sticking with the same method forever. But this is like trying to play just one game over and over and nothing else.

In *Self-Gamification Happiness Formula*, I call the *third* type of feedback system in a project game a "game-only" feedback system. I refer to it as such because I record the points, badges, and stars there as I make progress in what I set out to do during the day. I call the weekly calendar I use for it my "Points Gamebook" (other versions of this title are: "Points and Stars Gamebook" or "Points, Stars, and Badges Gamebook").

---

...

"Agile Project Management (APM) is an iterative process that focuses on customer value first, team interaction over tasks, and adapting to current business reality rather than following a prescriptive plan." — Julio Oliveira, *Scrum Simulation With Minecraft*

At first glance you might think this unnecessary, and that the points, badges, or stars would take too much time to record. But that is not the case.

You might already be using such "Point Gamebooks" without realising it, essentially playing a collecting game. You either need to collect the maximum number of points set or more than your competitors, or not go over the set limit or the time set. Habit trackers, which can be found in many commercial diaries, are an example of some of the elements of my "Points Gamebook." Or the steps on your step counter, giving you a point for each step. Or calories you count; they are points too.

Another example of this type is a gratitude journal, where you list all the things you are grateful for that day. If you write in such a journal, then consciously or subconsciously, your mind assesses the number of things you are grateful for on any given day, as soon as you recorded the last entry, as if you were evaluating a score. You might even find yourself checking how many listings you had the previous day and the day before.

And there are other examples. If you chose a writing project, then you will have word counts as your feedback system; if your activity is to learn to play a musical instrument, it would be the number of songs or pieces of music you have come to perform. And so on.

And another great feature of recording points for each completed task, especially the small ones, or ticking off each day you exercise or maintain another healthy habit, is that with each point and checkmark, you take a little moment to appreciate your effort. We often rely on the appreciation of others, but we won't be genuinely able to accept such praise if we can't appreciate what we do ourselves.

The *fourth* gamebook is the "Project Gamebook." That is just a notebook where I record all my thoughts for that project or write excerpts for my new books. Later I put those handwritten notes into digital format, which in itself could also be considered a digital "Project Gamebook."

Why do I bring up such a detailed, and perhaps strange, classification of the various ways we record what and when we want or have to do things, or the plans and content of what we create? I do so to draw your attention to how multi-faceted these project games are. Seeing your to-do lists, reports, Microsoft Excel sheets, road maps, your notes for the project, and the additional feedback system you might develop for yourself and your team members, like a multi-dimensional game (or even several games played at once), is a great key. This multidimensionality can add to the fun factor of each of your project and project management games.

My recommendation is that you test various approaches and observe what is right for you at any given time in your life. And continue the practice of seeing your projects like games, and yourself as their designer *and* player.

You can add game elements, like color codes, stars, and so on, to various types of entries in your Microsoft Excel sheets, or even sound effects to your PowerPoint presentation that contains the road map. You can even lay a flow chart in a project out like a board game and make progress visible through moving figurines along the board.

Of course, you would also need to record progress in another type of feedback system (one you have agreed with your customer or boss), but if these additional playful feedback plans will benefit you, your colleagues, and the project, then, by all means, create them and use them for your project games.

***An important note:*** Don't worry too much about recording your points precisely. Remember that although points, badges, and leaderboards provide a fun and effective reporting system, their primary role is to increase the fun you experience (such as, for example, the warm fuzziness you feel), not to keep an exact account. Keeping a precise account and fretting about the score will tear you out of the game and the fun experience.

**Your gameful epiphanies for today:**

# Day 20:
# Voluntary Participation in Gameful Project Management

**Reading time: 6 minutes**

"Finally, **voluntary participation** requires that everyone who is playing the game knowingly and willingly accepts the goal, the rules, and the feedback. Knowingness *establishes common ground* for multiple people to play together. And the freedom to enter or leave a game at will ensures that intentionally stressful and challenging work is experienced as *safe* and *pleasurable* activity." — Jane McGonigal, *Reality Is Broken*

Voluntary participation is the most important ingredient in the success of any project and any game. Successfully leaving a game that is not rewarding or a project that is going in the "wrong direction" can be meaningful too. It can also help you to return to it later. All of these are steps along the path unfolding in front of you, toward known or as yet unknown goals.

As you see in the definition above, voluntary participation is closely connected to goals, rules, and the way the feedback system is designed. So, if you see these three components as part of your game and do everything as a designer *and* player to keep them fun and efficient, then voluntary participation in your projects will become effortless.

In Self-Gamification, voluntary participation is multi-dimensional. It includes the will:

- to see your projects as games,
- to design and never stop developing these games (that includes the will to learn from other game and gamification designers; also those who practice Self-Gamification and approach project management, among other things, gamefully), and
- to play, in other words, actively engage in your Self-Motivational Games, in particular, your project and project management games.

These three components of voluntary participation are essential for you to keep turning your projects (and life) into games, if you wish to do so.

But there is also another, fourth dimension to voluntary participation in Self-Gamification and Gameful Project Management. "The freedom to enter and leave the game at will" is present in real-life projects too. It might not be as straightforward as it is in games, but each contract contains a clause of when a project will be canceled.

Besides that, you don't have to end a project altogether to be able to "leave" it for some time. We all have many projects to take care of. We go from one to another and then back to the first one. It is not that different from playing one game, leaving it for another (or something other than a game), and returning to it later.

Plus, if you stop recording points in your project's feedback system (especially the additional one for fun, with points, badges, stars, or gems), it isn't a problem at all - it doesn't mean you've lost anything, or that your projects (or life) will take a turn for the worse.

Some time after first turning my writing into a game, I forgot about it, but I still felt its positive effects. I suspect that I was still turning bits of my writing process into a game without recording the points. After all, I did have a feedback system in the form of word count, and chapters reviewed and edited.

Equally for you, if you stop recording points in a project, it doesn't have to mean you lose the fun you were previously experiencing. Even today, in some of my trickier projects, I use a simple feedback system (usually a tally on a scrap of paper) to get my work flowing, and as soon as it does, I stop recording the points and just enjoy doing the work. I call this quick and fun Self-Motivational Game design the "Project Booster."

So don't judge yourself if you notice that you aren't following the plans for your games to the letter. You still have all four components of voluntary participation if you actively engage in what you are doing and have fun.

But, if you notice yourself resisting and being "thrown out" of your game, then you can use the Self-Gamification (and Gameful Project Management) tools in your always-available toolset to address the fear, resentment, anger, or anything else that hinders you in your project games, boldly, honestly, and kindly.

There is a clear benefit to turning our lives into games, which is also the reason I keep playing. Resisting thoughts and the urge to procrastinate (including about things we think we really want to do) will never stop appearing, or becoming more sophisticated. This is probably why project management exists as an ever-evolving discipline.

These resisting thoughts might occur more rarely as we discover the fun in whatever we do, but there will always be a moment when our creative minds come up with some fretting ideas. In this case, Self-Gamification, and thus also Gameful Project Management, can help you turn the projects you fret about into Self-Motivational Games, in other words, real-life projects or activities that you love to engage in, both the design and the playing of.

When I got feedback from friends who had applied Self-Gamification, I realized something. Not only do Self-Motivational Games require voluntary participation for them to exist, both in design and play, but playing them facilitates voluntary participation in our lives' projects. It's an entirely rewarding "chicken and egg" causality dilemma, which helps us to experience work on our projects as a "safe and pleasurable activity."

Here is where the synergy of anthropology, kaizen, and gamification embraced by Self-Gamification and Gameful Project Management comes full circle.

So, for your project management games to be successful, you must be willing to see what you do as games, design them, and their rules, test the games, play them, follow the rules you have outlined, and through it all, be willing to have fun.

Please note, I don't mean that you should expect to have fun. It is easy to take suggestions from others and test out whether we like them or not, with the intention of proving them one way or another. But what makes a game or any activity enjoyable is first and foremost, the willingness to have fun.

That is the fifth and most important feature of voluntary participation in Self-Gamification and Gameful Project Management: the will to have fun.

**Your gameful epiphanies for today:**

# Day 21:
# Conclusions - Cultivating Gameful Project Management

## Reading time: 5 minutes

To summarize this book, which I hope served you as a useful and helpful awareness booster, here are a few thoughts on the aspect of cultivating Gameful Project Management. There is a fundamental wisdom to games, such as those we learned when we were small — those created for fun and to make their players happy.

These games are a safe place to be ourselves, to learn, to try something new, to challenge ourselves, without being judged, either by ourselves or others.

In this case, if a game can be designed to bring fun and happiness to its players, can't then any project or activity be re-designed to make them both fun and successful? Yes, they can.

Moreover, as both their designer and player, who is better placed than *you* to make them fun and engaging?

That is why it is so important to turn our real-life projects and, thus, also the management of them, into such fun games and safe spaces for us. We — and all the other players — will surpass any expectations.

The true goal of Gameful Project Management is for you to have fun and enjoy any of your projects and activities (including the management part of them) as if they were fun games. Or not even quite that. When you expect fun and concentrate too much on demanding it, you will end up not having fun. Being curious and open to discoveries is a goal worth aspiring to and practicing, as well as being willing to have fun too.

There are so many unexpected and fantastic possibilities when you turn whatever you do into fun games. These possibilities might be things you've never heard of or seen before, or you might have witnessed or experienced them before but do so now in new circumstances. Life is always surprising and can teach us something fresh in every moment. All we have to do is let it.

So, instead of resisting all the new information and all the surprises that come up in your projects, you can regard them as a game environment and yourself as a part of it. And suddenly it is easier to learn, to be open-minded, fully present, and resourceful.

Thus, when you enjoy designing and playing your projects, and the management of them, the growth mindset develops all by itself. You don't have to force it or be afraid that you don't have it.

I have realized that we humans are often afraid to be stalling and not moving forward, not growing. The truth is we do grow, every single moment. Especially if we are fully present in the moment of now, instead of hurrying somewhere. Don't beautiful flowers grow anchored to one spot? They do! Slowing down and enjoying every project and activity game can work wonders.

I recently discovered a brilliant and enlightening quote on slowing down. Here it is:

"Slowing down is just another way of waking up." — Elena Brower, author of *Art of Attention* and *Practice You*

So the whole trick is to slow down a little and be willing to see what you are doing as a game. It is also about getting inspired by "real" games or by anything that appears to be gameful or playful to you. Mind you, not something to disregard as a waste of time, but something you are eager to be great at, like your favorite game, which you both design *and* play.

Thanks to the Gameful Project Management (and Self-Gamification) approach, you can develop the ability to be aware (in other words, honest, kind, helpful, and non-judgmental toward yourself and others), to make small and effortless steps towards your goals, and last but not least, formulate the challenge and appreciate each of these small steps (develop and maintain the project game's goals, rules, and feedback system) in a fun, gameful way.

Cultivating Gameful Project Management means that you practice being honest, kind, and of service to all those involved in your projects, including yourself. You can identify the most appropriate next steps towards your goals and dreams. You design your own Self-Motivational Games (= your projects and activities turned into games), independent of whether you think you love doing or just "have to" do them. You have more and more fun in the process and, at some point, discover how much you enjoy "playing" and further developing (designing) them.

If you get frustrated and stuck again, you can repeat the following:

1. Become aware of where you are and where you want to head in any given task or project.

2. Identify the next smallest step that you can take with the least effort and resources to move forward.

3. Take and appreciate that step in whatever way you find fun and exciting.

Another great thing about Gameful Project Management is that your colleagues, managers, and customers become your allies in the project, not someone to resent or resist, but someone to learn from, cooperate with, share your experiences, and play with.

And now, all there is left for me to do is to wish you the following:

Enjoy your project games! Enjoy your project management quests!

And have fun designing, playing, and living!

## Your gameful epiphanies for today:

# Glossary

**Accountable:** "Someone who is accountable is completely responsible for what they do and must be able to give a satisfactory reason for it." — dictionary.cambridge.org/dictionary/english/accountable

**Agile Project Management:** "Agile Project Management (APM) is an iterative process that focuses on customer value first, team interaction over tasks, and adapting to current business reality rather than following a prescriptive plan." — Julio Oliveira, *Scrum Simulation With Minecraft*

**Anthropological Approach to Oneself:** "Practice your anthropological approach. Pretend you're a scientist observing a culture of one — yourself. The trick is not to judge what you see, but to neutrally observe how you function, including your thought processes. Awareness and kindness are key." — Ariel and Shya Kane, *How to Have A Match Made in Heaven*

**Anthropology:** "the scientific study of the origin, the behavior, and the physical, social, and cultural development of humans." — www.thefreedictionary.com/anthropology

**Ether:** "According to ancient and medieval science, aether (Ancient Greek: αἰθήρ, aithér), also spelled æther or ether and also called quintessence, is the material that fills the region of the universe above the terrestrial sphere. The concept of aether was used in several theories to explain several natural phenomena, such as the traveling of light and gravity. In the late 19th century, physicists postulated that aether permeated all throughout space, providing a medium through which light could travel in a vacuum, but evidence for the presence of such a medium was not found in the Michelson–Morley experiment, and this result has been interpreted as meaning that no such luminiferous aether exists." — en.wikipedia.org/wiki/Aether_(classical_element)

**Feedback System:** "The **feedback system** tells players how close they are to achieving the goal. It can take the form of points, levels, a score, or a progress bar. Or, in its most basic form, the feedback system can be as simple as the players' knowledge of an objective outcome: 'The game is over when . . .' Real-time feedback serves as a *promise* to the players that the goal is definitely achievable, and it provides *motivation* to keep playing." — Jane McGonigal, *Reality Is Broken*

**Flow:** "There is virtually nothing as engaging as this state of working at the very limits of your ability — or what both game designers and psychologists call 'flow.' When you are in a state of flow, you want to stay there: both quitting and winning are equally unsatisfying outcomes." — Jane McGonigal, *Reality is Broken*

**Fun:** "Fun is light, energetic, playful and...well...fun." — Will Wright in the foreword; "Fun is all about our brains feeling good — the release of endorphins into our system." "Fun is the act of mastering a problem mentally." "Fun is contextual." "Fun is another word for learning." — Raph Koster, *Theory of Fun for Game Design*

**Fun Detecting Antenna:** This extraordinary device is nothing more than awareness of whether you are experiencing fun, wherever you are, whatever, and however you are doing in any given moment of your life.

**Game:** "What defines a game are the goal, the rules, the feedback system, and voluntary participation. Everything else is an effort to reinforce and enhance these four core components." — Jane McGonigal, *Reality Is Broken*

**Game design:** "The art of applying design and aesthetics to create a game for entertainment or for educational, exercise, or experimental purposes. Increasingly, elements and principles of game design are also applied to other interactions, in the form of gamification." — en.wikipedia.org/wiki/Game_design

**Gameful:** "Playful, sportive; light-hearted; jesting, humorous." — www.lexico.com/en/definition/gameful

**Gameful Life:** "To lead a more gameful life, you simply have to be open to learning about the psychology of games—and be willing to experiment with new ways of thinking and acting that can help you increase your natural resilience." — Jane McGonigal, *SuperBetter*

**Gameful Project Management:** A way to approach project management gamefully, making it entertaining and fun. It is Self-Gamification focused on project management aspects.

**Gamification:** "The use of game design elements in non-game contexts" — Deterding, S., Dixon, D., Khaled, R., & Nacke, L. (2011). From game design elements to gamefulness: defining gamification. In Proceedings of the 15th international academic MindTrek conference: Envisioning future media environments (pp. 9-15). ACM.

**Goal:** "The **goal** is the specific outcome that players will work to achieve. It focuses their attention and continually orients their participation throughout the game. The goal provides players with *a sense of purpose.*" — Jane McGonigal, *Reality Is Broken*

**Inspiration:** "Inspiration is a feeling of enthusiasm you get from someone or something, which gives you new and creative ideas." — www.collinsdictionary.com/dictionary/english/inspiration

**Kaizen:** "Kaizen (改善) is the Japanese word for 'improvement.' In business, kaizen refers to activities that continuously improve all functions and involve all employees from the CEO to the assembly line workers. It also applies to processes, such as purchasing and logistics, that cross organizational boundaries into the supply chain. It has been applied in healthcare, psychotherapy, life-coaching, government, and banking. By improving standardized programmes and processes, kaizen aims to eliminate waste. Kaizen was first practiced in Japanese businesses after World War II, influenced in part by American business and quality-management teachers, and most notably as part of The Toyota Way. It has since spread throughout the world and has been applied to environments outside business and productivity." — en.wikipedia.org/wiki/Kaizen

**Komsomol:** "a political youth organization in the Soviet Union. It is sometimes described as the youth division of the Communist Party of the Soviet

Union (CPSU), although it was officially independent and referred to as 'the helper and the reserve of the CPSU'." — en.wikipedia.org/wiki/Komsomol

**Oktiabrionok:** "октябрёнок oktiabrionok (child between the ages of seven and eleven, in the first stages of Communist training)." — en.wikisource.org/wiki/Page:Dictionary_of_spoken_Russian_(1945).djvu/397

**Parable:** "A simple story told because it represents a basic moral truth or religious principle" — dictionary.cambridge.org/dictionary/english/parable

**Project Management:** "The deliberate planning, control, and coordination of all aspects of a project (initiating, planning, executing, controlling, and closing), in order to achieve the agreed objectives." — www.oxfordreference.com/view/10.1093/oi/authority.20110803100349325

**Project Management Gamification:** The process of bringing game elements into project management processes.

**Project Management Institute:** "Founded in 1969, the Project Management Institute (PMI) sets standards for the project management profession. It has 454,000 members in 180 countries." — Kory

Kogon, Suzette Blakemore, James Wood, *Project Management for the Unofficial Project Manager*

**Role-Playing Game:** "A role-playing game (sometimes spelled roleplaying game; abbreviated RPG) is a game in which players assume the roles of characters in a fictional setting. Players take responsibility for acting out these roles within a narrative, either through literal acting, or through a process of structured decision-making regarding character development. Actions taken within many games succeed or fail according to a formal system of rules and guidelines." — en.wikipedia.org/wiki/Role-playing_game

**Rules:** "The **rules** place limitations on how players can achieve the goal. By removing or limiting the obvious ways of getting to the goal, the rules push players to explore previous uncharted possibility spaces. They *unleash creativity* and *foster strategic thinking*." — Jane McGonigal, *Reality Is Broken*

**SCRUM:** "Nowadays Scrum is considered the most adopted agile project management framework around the world." — Julio Oliveira, *Scrum Simulation With Minecraft*

**Self-Gamification:** Self-Gamification is the art of turning our own lives into games. It is the application of game design elements to our own lives. Self-Gamification is a self-help approach showing us how to be playful and gameful, and bringing anthropology, kaizen, and gamification-based methods together. In Self-Gamification, we are both the designers *and* the players of our Self-Motivational Games. Self-Gamification is about creating uplifting emotions for ourselves and keeping ourselves "happily entertained" with whatever comes our way in our lives. Thus, Self-Gamification equals approaching life gamefully.

**Self-Motivational Game:** A real-life project or activity that you adjust in such a way that it feels like a fun game, with which you are eager and happy to engage, both in terms of its design and the playing of it.

**Serious Games:** "Full games that have been created for reasons other than pure entertainment." — Andrzej Marczewski, *Even Ninja Monkeys Like to Play: Unicorn Edition*

**Serious Games for Project Management:** Full games created often to educate in the project management subject.

**Unofficial Project Manager:** "If most of your work time is spent on projects and you've never been exposed to formal project management training, you are an unofficial project manager." — Kory Kogon, Suzette Blakemore, James Wood, *Project Management for the Unofficial Project Manager*

**Voluntary Participation:** "Finally, **voluntary participation** requires that everyone who is playing the game knowingly and willingly accepts the goal, the rules, and the feedback. Knowingness *establishes common ground* for multiple people to play together. And the freedom to enter or leave a game at will ensures that intentionally stressful and challenging work is experienced as *safe* and *pleasurable* activity."
— Jane McGonigal, *Reality Is Broken*

**Young pioneers:** "a mass youth organization of the Soviet Union for children of age 9–15 that existed between 1922 and 1991. Similar to the Scouting organizations of the Western world, Pioneers learned skills of social cooperation and attended publicly funded summer camps." — en.wikipedia.org/wiki/Vladimir_Lenin_All-Union_Pioneer_Organization

# Acronyms

FDA = Fun Detecting Antenna
GB = Gamebook
GPM = Gameful Project Management
PGB = Project Gamebook
SG = Self-Gamification
SMG = Self-Motivational Game

P.S. These are just some of the acronyms I use, and which you could too. I didn't use them in the text of the book, but they are fun to apply when making notes on my SMG designs and plans. I invite you to create your own terms, game names, acronyms, and abbreviations. Approach these like everything else in GPM, gamefully and playfully.

# Further Reading

Note: this list contains both resources I have referred to in the book, and others that I consider inspiring and nurturing for project managers, both official and unofficial. Each list below is sorted alphabetically.

**Sources with tools on awareness and anthropological (= non-judgmental) seeing**

- *Anthropology For Dummies*, Cameron M. Smith, 2009
- *Being Here: Modern Day Tales of Enlightenment*, Ariel and Shya Kane, 2007
- *Being Here...Too: Short Stories of Modern Day Enlightenment*, Ariel and Shya Kane, 2018
- *Practical Enlightenment*, Ariel and Shya Kane, 2015
- *Working on Yourself Doesn't Work: The 3 Simple Ideas That Will Instantaneously Transform Your Life*, Ariel and Shya Kane, 2008

**Books on kaizen and small steps:**

- *One Small Step Can Change Your Life: The Kaizen Way*, Robert Maurer, 2014

- *Mastering Fear: Harnessing Emotion to Achieve Excellence in Work*, Health and Relationships, Robert Maurer, 2016
- *The Spirit of Kaizen: Creating Lasting Excellence One Small Step at a Time*, Robert Maurer, 2012

## Books on game design and gamification (and also project management):

- *Actionable Gamification: Beyond Points, Badges, and Leaderboards*, Yu-kai Chou, 2015
- *For the Win: How Game Thinking Can Revolutionize Your Business*, Kevin Werbach and Dan Hunter
- *Game Project Completed: How Successful Indie Game Developers Finish Their Projects*, Thomas Schwarzl, 2014
- *Game Thinking: Innovate Smarter & Drive Deep Engagement with Design Techniques from Hit Games*, Amy Jo Kim, 2018
- *Lifelong Kindergarten: Cultivating Creativity through Projects, Passion, Peers, and Play*, Mitchel Resnick, 2017
- *Reality Is Broken: Why Games Make Us Better and How They Can Change the World*, Jane McGonigal, 2011
- *Scrum Simulation With Minecraft: A Gamified Approach to Teach Agile Project Management*, Julio Oliveira, 2016

- *SuperBetter: The Power of Living Gamefully*, Jane McGonigal, 2015
- *The Game Inventor's Guidebook: How to Invent and Sell Board Games, Card Games, Role-playing Games & Everything in Between!*, Brian Tinsman, 2008
- *Theory of Fun for Game Design*, Raph Koster, 2013

**Books on project management, everyday courage, and mastering work and business life in rewarding ways:**

- *Project Management for the Unofficial Project Manager*, Kory Kogon, Suzette Blakemore, James Wood, 2015
- *The 5 Second Rule: Transform Your Life, Work, and Confidence with Everyday Courage*, Mel Robbins, 2017
- *The Go-Giver: A Little Story About a Powerful Business Idea*, Bob Burg and John David Mann, 2010
- *The Go-Giver Influencer: A Little Story About a Most Persuasive Idea*, Bob Burg and John David Mann, 2018
- *The Go-Giver Leader: A Little Story About What Matters Most in Business*, Bob Burg and John David Mann, 2016
- *The Latte Factor: Why You Don't Have to Be Rich to Live Rich*, David Bach and John David Mann, 2019

# Acknowledgments

First of all, dear reader, thank you very much for purchasing and reading *Gameful Project Management*!

I hope you enjoyed reading this book as much as I loved writing it.

Of all the people I want to thank for supporting me and affecting the outcome of this book, I would like to start with my sister, Svetlana Breum, to whom this book is dedicated. Dearest Svetlana, you are one of the most passionate and gameful project managers I know. The way you master challenges in your life has always been utterly inspiring to me. Your excellence, humor, and mastery were always something I looked up to. You were always one of my biggest role models, before, and especially after, our father died. And you still are. Thank you for sharing the games you use when educating others about project management and other disciplines. Thank you for the nights we spent together preparing for jobs and exams. I will always treasure my memories of them. Thank you for being you! Te iubesc, Svetuli!

Big and heartfelt thanks go to my mother, Veronica Ichizli, who not only brought me up but has served as a frank and caring consultant in many of my projects since childhood. Iti multumesc din inima, draga Mama!

A huge thank you to one of my sister's dearest friends, and now also mine, Patricia Orlowitz. After not seeing each other for twenty years, she came to Denmark to visit my sister, her daughter, and all our families in September 2019. During our sightseeing tour of Aalborg, Patricia and I had lunch together and I shared my projects and especially Gameful Project Management with her. Dear Patricia, thank you so much for your sincere interest and encouragement, and for sharing your experiences of working in the field of project and business development and management.

A shout out to my dear friends Katja Dietermann and Meike Schmigale, with whom I had the pleasure of eating lunch during the "Transformation in The Workplace" seminar in Hamburg, with award-winning authors, and dear friends, Ariel and Shya Kane, in October 2019. Dear Katja and Meike, thank you so much for your interest and also challenging me on what I had to share about Gameful Project Management. After our lunch I became aware of what I wanted to convey with this book. Our conversation helped me to realize that what I was writing here was an awareness booster on the new tools "Gameful Life" provides, rather than a new approach to replace hundreds of years of knowledge on project management, developed by generations.

I am immensely grateful to Alice Jago for editing this book. You make every book you edit, including this one, sound so much more beautiful. And thank you so much for making the book cover. I love working with you, Alice!

My biggest thanks go to my husband, Michael, and our children Niklas and Emma. I wouldn't be able to turn my life into fun games without your loving encouragement, or you challenging me in the most exciting and brilliant ways. Without you, this book (and the rest of my heart's projects) would not be a reality. I love you!

# About the Author

Victoria is a writer, coach, and consultant with a background in semiconductor physics, electronic engineering (with a Ph.D.), information technology, and business development. While being a non-gamer, Victoria came up with the term *Self-Gamification*, a gameful and playful self-help approach bringing anthropology, kaizen, and gamification-based methods together to increase the quality of life. She approaches all areas of her life this way. Due to the fun she has turning everything in her life into games, she intends to never stop designing and playing them.

Victoria is the author of the *Self-Gamification Happiness Formula* and *5 Minute Perseverance Game*, as well as the instructor of the online course *Motivate Yourself by Turning Your Life Into Fun Games*. *Gameful Project Management* is Victoria's fourth work on how to approach projects, project management, and life with excellence and ease in a gameful way — the Self-Gamification way.

Victoria was born in Moldova, lived in Germany for twelve years, and now lives in

Aalborg, Denmark, with her husband and two children.

Visit or contact Victoria at victoriaichizlibartels.com or optimistwriter.com.

Subscribe to Victoria's blog and news at www.victoriaichizlibartels.com/subscribe-to-victorias-blog/.

To read about and join the Self-Gamification community go to www.victoriaichizlibartels.com/community/.

# Also by Victoria Ichizli-Bartels

### *Motivational Books*

*Self-Gamification Happiness Formula:*
*How to Turn Your Life into Fun Games*

*5 Minute Perseverance Game:*
*Play Daily for a Month and Become the Ultimate Procrastination Breaker*

*Cheerleading for Writers:*
*Discover How Truly Talented You Are*

*Turn Your No Into Yes:*
*15 Yes-Or-No Questions to Disentangle Your Project*
Free e-book
(Available upon subscription to victoriaichizlibartels.com or optimistwriter.com)

### *Online Course on Udemy*

*Motivate Yourself by Turning Your Life Into Fun Games:*
*Practice Self-Gamification, a Unique Self-Help Approach Uniting Anthropology, Kaizen, and Gamification*

## *Business Books*

*Take Control of Your Business:*
*Learn what Business Rules are, discover that you are already using them, then update them to maximize your business success*

### *Resources*

*The Business Rules Memo*
www.victoriaichizlibartels.com/s1000d-navigation-maps/#BrMemo

## *S1000D Books*

**brDoc, BREX, and Co.: S1000D Business Rules Made Easier**

*S1000D® Issue 4.1 and Issue 4.2 Navigation Map:*
*552+87 and 427+90 Business Rule Decision Points Arranged into two Linear Topic Maps to Facilitate Learning, Understanding, and Implementation of S1000D®*

*S1000D Issue 4.1 Untangled:*
*552+ Business Rules Decision Points Arranged into a Linear Topic Map to Facilitate Learning, Understanding and Implementation of S1000D*
(unpublished, replaced by *S1000D® Issue 4.1 and Issue 4.2 Navigation Map,* see above)

### *Data Sheets and Templates*

*S1000D® Navigation Maps*
www.victoriaichizlibartels.com/s1000d-navigation-maps/

## *Fiction*
## *Books*

*Between Grace and Abyss: A Short Story*
(Also available as a free e-book upon subscription to
victoriaichizlibartels.com or optimistwriter.com)

*Nothing Is As It Seems: A Novelette*
(The e-book is permanently free)

*Seven Broken Pieces: A short story*
(Prequel to series "A Life Upside Down")

*A Spy's Daughter: A novella*
(Book 1 in series "A Life Upside Down")

*The Truth About Family:*
*A novel inspired by true events*